Welcome to Our Humble Commode!

PLEASE SIGN OUR GUEST BOOK.
IT'S SOMETHING TO DO,
WHILE YOU DO WHAT YOU DOO.

Welcome! PLEASE SEAT YOURSELF AND ENJOY YOUR VISIT!

NAME: _____ DATE: _____ TIME: _____ DURATION OF VISIT: _____
HRS   MIN   SEC

PURPOSE FOR VISIT: ☐ #1 ☐ #2 ☐ OTHER: _____ SUCCESS? ☐ YES ☐ NO

FAVORITE EUPHEMISM FOR PERFORMING #1:

FAVORITE RESTROOM GRAFFITI OR YOUR ORIGNAL DOODLE:

FAVORITE EUPHEMISM FOR PERFORMING #2:

WHILE YOU WERE HERE, DID YOU:
☐ TEXT SOMEONE
☐ MAKE A PHONE CALL
☐ EMAIL
☐ CHECK SOCIAL MEDIA
☐ TAKE A SELFIE
☐ LOOK IN THE MEDICINE CABINET
☐ CHECK YOUR TEETH
☐ CHECK OUT YOUR BUTT
☐ CHECK YOUR FLY
☐ READ
☐ FIX YOUR HAIR
☐ TAKE SOME EXTRA "ME TIME"
☐ TALK TO YOURSELF
☐ CONDUCT BUSINESS OTHER THAN YOUR "BUSINESS." CARE TO SHARE?
_____

FAVORITE NAME FOR THIS ROOM:
☐ BATHROOM   ☐ JOHN
☐ TOILET   ☐ CAN
☐ POWDER ROOM   ☐ HEAD
☐ LAVATORY   ☐ POTTY
☐ SHITTER   ☐ CRAPPER
☐ LOO   ☐ WC
☐ LITTLE GIRLS ROOM
☐ LITTLE BOYS ROOM
☐ COMFORT STATION
☐ OTHER: _____
_____
_____

THOUGHTS/MESSAGES: _____
_____
_____

RATINGS:
	1	2	3	4	5
CLEANLINESS	☆	☆	☆	☆	☆
AMBIENCE	☆	☆	☆	☆	☆
AMENITIES	☆	☆	☆	☆	☆
SOUND PROOFING	☆	☆	☆	☆	☆
QUALITY OF THE FLUSH	☆	☆	☆	☆	☆
TOILET PAPER	☆	☆	☆	☆	☆

OVERALL EXPERIENCE:
☐ BEST SEAT IN THE HOUSE ★ ★ ★ ★ ★
☐ WOULD POOP HERE AGAIN ★ ★ ★ ★
☐ SHIT GOT REAL ★ ★ ★
☐ SAME SHIT DIFFERENT HOUSE ★ ★
☐ THINGS JUST DIDN'T COME OUT RIGHT ★

Welcome! PLEASE SEAT YOURSELF AND ENJOY YOUR VISIT!

NAME: _____ DATE: _____ TIME: _____ DURATION OF VISIT: _____
HRS   MIN   SEC

PURPOSE FOR VISIT: ☐ #1 ☐ #2 ☐ OTHER: _____ SUCCESS? ☐ YES ☐ NO

FAVORITE EUPHEMISM FOR PERFORMING #1:

FAVORITE RESTROOM GRAFFITI OR YOUR ORIGNAL DOODLE:

FAVORITE EUPHEMISM FOR PERFORMING #2:

WHILE YOU WERE HERE, DID YOU:
☐ TEXT SOMEONE
☐ MAKE A PHONE CALL
☐ EMAIL
☐ CHECK SOCIAL MEDIA
☐ TAKE A SELFIE
☐ LOOK IN THE MEDICINE CABINET
☐ CHECK YOUR TEETH
☐ CHECK OUT YOUR BUTT
☐ CHECK YOUR FLY
☐ READ
☐ FIX YOUR HAIR
☐ TAKE SOME EXTRA "ME TIME"
☐ TALK TO YOURSELF
☐ CONDUCT BUSINESS OTHER THAN YOUR "BUSINESS." CARE TO SHARE?
_____

FAVORITE NAME FOR THIS ROOM:
☐ BATHROOM   ☐ JOHN
☐ TOILET   ☐ CAN
☐ POWDER ROOM   ☐ HEAD
☐ LAVATORY   ☐ POTTY
☐ SHITTER   ☐ CRAPPER
☐ LOO   ☐ WC
☐ LITTLE GIRLS ROOM
☐ LITTLE BOYS ROOM
☐ COMFORT STATION
☐ OTHER: _____
_____

RATINGS: 1 2 3 4 5
CLEANLINESS   ☆ ☆ ☆ ☆ ☆
AMBIENCE   ☆ ☆ ☆ ☆ ☆
AMENITIES   ☆ ☆ ☆ ☆ ☆
SOUND PROOFING   ☆ ☆ ☆ ☆ ☆
QUALITY OF THE FLUSH ☆ ☆ ☆ ☆ ☆
TOILET PAPER   ☆ ☆ ☆ ☆ ☆

OVERALL EXPERIENCE:
☐ BEST SEAT IN THE HOUSE   ★ ★ ★ ★ ★
☐ WOULD POOP HERE AGAIN   ★ ★ ★ ★
☐ SHIT GOT REAL   ★ ★ ★
☐ SAME SHIT DIFFERENT HOUSE   ★ ★
☐ THINGS JUST DIDN'T COME OUT RIGHT ★

THOUGHTS/MESSAGES: _____
_____
_____

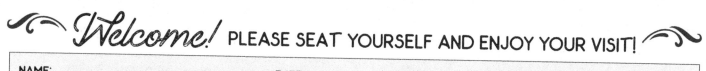

Welcome! PLEASE SEAT YOURSELF AND ENJOY YOUR VISIT!

NAME: _____ DATE: _____ TIME: _____ DURATION OF VISIT: _____

HRS   MIN   SEC

PURPOSE FOR VISIT: ▢ #1 ▢ #2 ▢ OTHER: _____ SUCCESS? ▢ YES ▢ NO

FAVORITE EUPHEMISM FOR PERFORMING #1:

FAVORITE EUPHEMISM FOR PERFORMING #2:

FAVORITE RESTROOM GRAFFITI OR YOUR ORIGNAL DOODLE:

WHILE YOU WERE HERE, DID YOU:
▢ TEXT SOMEONE
▢ MAKE A PHONE CALL
▢ EMAIL
▢ CHECK SOCIAL MEDIA
▢ TAKE A SELFIE
▢ LOOK IN THE MEDICINE CABINET
▢ CHECK YOUR TEETH
▢ CHECK OUT YOUR BUTT
▢ CHECK YOUR FLY
▢ READ
▢ FIX YOUR HAIR
▢ TAKE SOME EXTRA "ME TIME"
▢ TALK TO YOURSELF
▢ CONDUCT BUSINESS OTHER THAN YOUR "BUSINESS." CARE TO SHARE?

FAVORITE NAME FOR THIS ROOM:
▢ BATHROOM
▢ TOILET
▢ POWDER ROOM
▢ LAVATORY
▢ SHITTER
▢ LOO
▢ LITTLE GIRLS ROOM
▢ LITTLE BOYS ROOM
▢ COMFORT STATION
▢ OTHER: _____
_____

▢ JOHN
▢ CAN
▢ HEAD
▢ POTTY
▢ CRAPPER
▢ WC

RATINGS:
	1	2	3	4	5
CLEANLINESS	☆	☆	☆	☆	☆
AMBIENCE	☆	☆	☆	☆	☆
AMENITIES	☆	☆	☆	☆	☆
SOUND PROOFING	☆	☆	☆	☆	☆
QUALITY OF THE FLUSH	☆	☆	☆	☆	☆
TOILET PAPER	☆	☆	☆	☆	☆

OVERALL EXPERIENCE:
▢ BEST SEAT IN THE HOUSE ★ ★ ★ ★ ★
▢ WOULD POOP HERE AGAIN ★ ★ ★ ★
▢ SHIT GOT REAL ★ ★ ★
▢ SAME SHIT DIFFERENT HOUSE ★ ★
▢ THINGS JUST DIDN'T COME OUT RIGHT ★

THOUGHTS/MESSAGES: _____
_____
_____

Welcome! PLEASE SEAT YOURSELF AND ENJOY YOUR VISIT!

NAME: _____ DATE: _____ TIME: _____ DURATION OF VISIT: _____
HRS   MIN   SEC

PURPOSE FOR VISIT: ▢ #1 ▢ #2 ▢ OTHER: _____ SUCCESS? ▢ YES ▢ NO

FAVORITE EUPHEMISM FOR PERFORMING #1:

FAVORITE RESTROOM GRAFFITI OR YOUR ORIGNAL DOODLE:

FAVORITE EUPHEMISM FOR PERFORMING #2:

WHILE YOU WERE HERE, DID YOU:
- ☐ TEXT SOMEONE
- ☐ MAKE A PHONE CALL
- ☐ EMAIL
- ☐ CHECK SOCIAL MEDIA
- ☐ TAKE A SELFIE
- ☐ LOOK IN THE MEDICINE CABINET
- ☐ CHECK YOUR TEETH
- ☐ CHECK OUT YOUR BUTT
- ☐ CHECK YOUR FLY
- ☐ READ
- ☐ FIX YOUR HAIR
- ☐ TAKE SOME EXTRA "ME TIME"
- ☐ TALK TO YOURSELF
- ☐ CONDUCT BUSINESS OTHER THAN YOUR "BUSINESS." CARE TO SHARE?
  _____

FAVORITE NAME FOR THIS ROOM:
- ☐ BATHROOM
- ☐ TOILET
- ☐ POWDER ROOM
- ☐ LAVATORY
- ☐ SHITTER
- ☐ LOO
- ☐ LITTLE GIRLS ROOM
- ☐ LITTLE BOYS ROOM
- ☐ COMFORT STATION
- ☐ OTHER: _____
- ☐ JOHN
- ☐ CAN
- ☐ HEAD
- ☐ POTTY
- ☐ CRAPPER
- ☐ WC

RATINGS: 1 2 3 4 5
CLEANLINESS   ☆ ☆ ☆ ☆ ☆
AMBIENCE   ☆ ☆ ☆ ☆ ☆
AMENITIES   ☆ ☆ ☆ ☆ ☆
SOUND PROOFING   ☆ ☆ ☆ ☆ ☆
QUALITY OF THE FLUSH ☆ ☆ ☆ ☆ ☆
TOILET PAPER   ☆ ☆ ☆ ☆ ☆

OVERALL EXPERIENCE:
- ☐ BEST SEAT IN THE HOUSE   ★ ★ ★ ★ ★
- ☐ WOULD POOP HERE AGAIN   ★ ★ ★ ★
- ☐ SHIT GOT REAL   ★ ★ ★
- ☐ SAME SHIT DIFFERENT HOUSE   ★ ★
- ☐ THINGS JUST DIDN'T COME OUT RIGHT ★

THOUGHTS/MESSAGES: _____
_____
_____

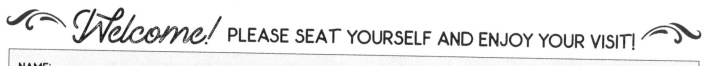

Welcome! PLEASE SEAT YOURSELF AND ENJOY YOUR VISIT!

NAME: _____ DATE: _____ TIME: _____ DURATION OF VISIT: _____
HRS   MIN   SEC

PURPOSE FOR VISIT: ▢ #1 ▢ #2 ▢ OTHER: _____ SUCCESS? ▢ YES ▢ NO

FAVORITE EUPHEMISM FOR PERFORMING #1:

FAVORITE RESTROOM GRAFFITI OR YOUR ORIGNAL DOODLE:

FAVORITE EUPHEMISM FOR PERFORMING #2:

WHILE YOU WERE HERE, DID YOU:
☐ TEXT SOMEONE
☐ MAKE A PHONE CALL
☐ EMAIL
☐ CHECK SOCIAL MEDIA
☐ TAKE A SELFIE
☐ LOOK IN THE MEDICINE CABINET
☐ CHECK YOUR TEETH
☐ CHECK OUT YOUR BUTT
☐ CHECK YOUR FLY
☐ READ
☐ FIX YOUR HAIR
☐ TAKE SOME EXTRA "ME TIME"
☐ TALK TO YOURSELF
☐ CONDUCT BUSINESS OTHER THAN YOUR "BUSINESS." CARE TO SHARE?
_____

FAVORITE NAME FOR THIS ROOM:
☐ BATHROOM   ☐ JOHN
☐ TOILET   ☐ CAN
☐ POWDER ROOM   ☐ HEAD
☐ LAVATORY   ☐ POTTY
☐ SHITTER   ☐ CRAPPER
☐ LOO   ☐ WC
☐ LITTLE GIRLS ROOM
☐ LITTLE BOYS ROOM
☐ COMFORT STATION
☐ OTHER: _____
_____

THOUGHTS/MESSAGES: _____
_____
_____

RATINGS:
	1	2	3	4	5
CLEANLINESS	☆	☆	☆	☆	☆
AMBIENCE	☆	☆	☆	☆	☆
AMENITIES	☆	☆	☆	☆	☆
SOUND PROOFING	☆	☆	☆	☆	☆
QUALITY OF THE FLUSH	☆	☆	☆	☆	☆
TOILET PAPER	☆	☆	☆	☆	☆

OVERALL EXPERIENCE:
☐ BEST SEAT IN THE HOUSE ★ ★ ★ ★ ★
☐ WOULD POOP HERE AGAIN ★ ★ ★ ★
☐ SHIT GOT REAL ★ ★ ★
☐ SAME SHIT DIFFERENT HOUSE ★ ★
☐ THINGS JUST DIDN'T COME OUT RIGHT ★

Welcome! PLEASE SEAT YOURSELF AND ENJOY YOUR VISIT!

NAME: _____ DATE: _____ TIME: _____ DURATION OF VISIT: _____
HRS   MIN   SEC

PURPOSE FOR VISIT: ☐ #1 ☐ #2 ☐ OTHER: _____ SUCCESS? ☐ YES ☐ NO

FAVORITE EUPHEMISM FOR PERFORMING #1:

FAVORITE EUPHEMISM FOR PERFORMING #2:

FAVORITE RESTROOM GRAFFITI OR YOUR ORIGNAL DOODLE:

WHILE YOU WERE HERE, DID YOU:
☐ TEXT SOMEONE
☐ MAKE A PHONE CALL
☐ EMAIL
☐ CHECK SOCIAL MEDIA
☐ TAKE A SELFIE
☐ LOOK IN THE MEDICINE CABINET
☐ CHECK YOUR TEETH
☐ CHECK OUT YOUR BUTT
☐ CHECK YOUR FLY
☐ READ
☐ FIX YOUR HAIR
☐ TAKE SOME EXTRA "ME TIME"
☐ TALK TO YOURSELF
☐ CONDUCT BUSINESS OTHER THAN YOUR "BUSINESS." CARE TO SHARE?
_____

FAVORITE NAME FOR THIS ROOM:
☐ BATHROOM
☐ TOILET
☐ POWDER ROOM
☐ LAVATORY
☐ SHITTER
☐ LOO
☐ LITTLE GIRLS ROOM
☐ LITTLE BOYS ROOM
☐ COMFORT STATION
☐ OTHER: _____
_____

☐ JOHN
☐ CAN
☐ HEAD
☐ POTTY
☐ CRAPPER
☐ WC

RATINGS: 1 2 3 4 5
CLEANLINESS   ☆ ☆ ☆ ☆ ☆
AMBIENCE   ☆ ☆ ☆ ☆ ☆
AMENITIES   ☆ ☆ ☆ ☆ ☆
SOUND PROOFING   ☆ ☆ ☆ ☆ ☆
QUALITY OF THE FLUSH   ☆ ☆ ☆ ☆ ☆
TOILET PAPER   ☆ ☆ ☆ ☆ ☆

OVERALL EXPERIENCE:
☐ BEST SEAT IN THE HOUSE   ★ ★ ★ ★ ★
☐ WOULD POOP HERE AGAIN   ★ ★ ★ ★
☐ SHIT GOT REAL   ★ ★ ★
☐ SAME SHIT DIFFERENT HOUSE   ★ ★
☐ THINGS JUST DIDN'T COME OUT RIGHT   ★

THOUGHTS/MESSAGES: _____
_____
_____

Welcome! PLEASE SEAT YOURSELF AND ENJOY YOUR VISIT!

NAME: _____ DATE: _____ TIME: _____ DURATION OF VISIT: _____
HRS   MIN   SEC

PURPOSE FOR VISIT: ⬜ #1 ⬜ #2 ⬜ OTHER: _____ SUCCESS? ⬜ YES ⬜ NO

FAVORITE EUPHEMISM FOR PERFORMING #1:

FAVORITE EUPHEMISM FOR PERFORMING #2:

FAVORITE RESTROOM GRAFFITI OR YOUR ORIGNAL DOODLE:

WHILE YOU WERE HERE, DID YOU:
- ⬜ TEXT SOMEONE
- ⬜ MAKE A PHONE CALL
- ⬜ EMAIL
- ⬜ CHECK SOCIAL MEDIA
- ⬜ TAKE A SELFIE
- ⬜ LOOK IN THE MEDICINE CABINET
- ⬜ CHECK YOUR TEETH
- ⬜ CHECK OUT YOUR BUTT
- ⬜ CHECK YOUR FLY
- ⬜ READ
- ⬜ FIX YOUR HAIR
- ⬜ TAKE SOME EXTRA "ME TIME"
- ⬜ TALK TO YOURSELF
- ⬜ CONDUCT BUSINESS OTHER THAN YOUR "BUSINESS." CARE TO SHARE?

FAVORITE NAME FOR THIS ROOM:
- ⬜ BATHROOM
- ⬜ TOILET
- ⬜ POWDER ROOM
- ⬜ LAVATORY
- ⬜ SHITTER
- ⬜ LOO
- ⬜ LITTLE GIRLS ROOM
- ⬜ LITTLE BOYS ROOM
- ⬜ COMFORT STATION
- ⬜ OTHER: _____

- ⬜ JOHN
- ⬜ CAN
- ⬜ HEAD
- ⬜ POTTY
- ⬜ CRAPPER
- ⬜ WC

THOUGHTS/MESSAGES: _____

RATINGS:
	1	2	3	4	5
CLEANLINESS	☆	☆	☆	☆	☆
AMBIENCE	☆	☆	☆	☆	☆
AMENITIES	☆	☆	☆	☆	☆
SOUND PROOFING	☆	☆	☆	☆	☆
QUALITY OF THE FLUSH	☆	☆	☆	☆	☆
TOILET PAPER	☆	☆	☆	☆	☆

OVERALL EXPERIENCE:
- ⬜ BEST SEAT IN THE HOUSE ★ ★ ★ ★ ★
- ⬜ WOULD POOP HERE AGAIN ★ ★ ★ ★
- ⬜ SHIT GOT REAL ★ ★ ★
- ⬜ SAME SHIT DIFFERENT HOUSE ★ ★
- ⬜ THINGS JUST DIDN'T COME OUT RIGHT ★

Welcome! PLEASE SEAT YOURSELF AND ENJOY YOUR VISIT!

NAME: _____ DATE: _____ TIME: _____ DURATION OF VISIT: _____
HRS   MIN   SEC

PURPOSE FOR VISIT: ☐ #1 ☐ #2 ☐ OTHER: _____ SUCCESS? ☐ YES ☐ NO

FAVORITE EUPHEMISM FOR PERFORMING #1:

FAVORITE RESTROOM GRAFFITI OR YOUR ORIGNAL DOODLE:

FAVORITE EUPHEMISM FOR PERFORMING #2:

WHILE YOU WERE HERE, DID YOU:
☐ TEXT SOMEONE
☐ MAKE A PHONE CALL
☐ EMAIL
☐ CHECK SOCIAL MEDIA
☐ TAKE A SELFIE
☐ LOOK IN THE MEDICINE CABINET
☐ CHECK YOUR TEETH
☐ CHECK OUT YOUR BUTT
☐ CHECK YOUR FLY
☐ READ
☐ FIX YOUR HAIR
☐ TAKE SOME EXTRA "ME TIME"
☐ TALK TO YOURSELF
☐ CONDUCT BUSINESS OTHER THAN YOUR "BUSINESS." CARE TO SHARE?
_____

FAVORITE NAME FOR THIS ROOM:
☐ BATHROOM   ☐ JOHN
☐ TOILET   ☐ CAN
☐ POWDER ROOM   ☐ HEAD
☐ LAVATORY   ☐ POTTY
☐ SHITTER   ☐ CRAPPER
☐ LOO   ☐ WC
☐ LITTLE GIRLS ROOM
☐ LITTLE BOYS ROOM
☐ COMFORT STATION
☐ OTHER: _____
_____

THOUGHTS/MESSAGES: _____
_____
_____

RATINGS:
	1	2	3	4	5
CLEANLINESS	☆	☆	☆	☆	☆
AMBIENCE	☆	☆	☆	☆	☆
AMENITIES	☆	☆	☆	☆	☆
SOUND PROOFING	☆	☆	☆	☆	☆
QUALITY OF THE FLUSH	☆	☆	☆	☆	☆
TOILET PAPER	☆	☆	☆	☆	☆

OVERALL EXPERIENCE:
☐ BEST SEAT IN THE HOUSE ★★★★★
☐ WOULD POOP HERE AGAIN ★★★★
☐ SHIT GOT REAL ★★★
☐ SAME SHIT DIFFERENT HOUSE ★★
☐ THINGS JUST DIDN'T COME OUT RIGHT ★

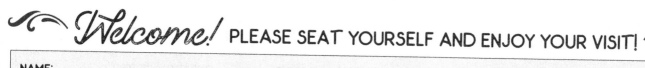

Welcome! PLEASE SEAT YOURSELF AND ENJOY YOUR VISIT!

NAME: _____ DATE: _____ TIME: _____ DURATION OF VISIT: _____
HRS   MIN   SEC

PURPOSE FOR VISIT: ☐ #1   ☐ #2   ☐ OTHER: _____   SUCCESS? ☐ YES ☐ NO

FAVORITE EUPHEMISM FOR PERFORMING #1:   FAVORITE RESTROOM GRAFFITI OR YOUR ORIGNAL DOODLE:

FAVORITE EUPHEMISM FOR PERFORMING #2:

WHILE YOU WERE HERE, DID YOU:
☐ TEXT SOMEONE
☐ MAKE A PHONE CALL
☐ EMAIL
☐ CHECK SOCIAL MEDIA
☐ TAKE A SELFIE
☐ LOOK IN THE MEDICINE CABINET
☐ CHECK YOUR TEETH
☐ CHECK OUT YOUR BUTT
☐ CHECK YOUR FLY
☐ READ
☐ FIX YOUR HAIR
☐ TAKE SOME EXTRA "ME TIME"
☐ TALK TO YOURSELF
☐ CONDUCT BUSINESS OTHER THAN YOUR "BUSINESS." CARE TO SHARE?

FAVORITE NAME FOR THIS ROOM:
☐ BATHROOM   ☐ JOHN
☐ TOILET   ☐ CAN
☐ POWDER ROOM   ☐ HEAD
☐ LAVATORY   ☐ POTTY
☐ SHITTER   ☐ CRAPPER
☐ LOO   ☐ WC
☐ LITTLE GIRLS ROOM
☐ LITTLE BOYS ROOM
☐ COMFORT STATION
☐ OTHER: _____

_____

THOUGHTS/MESSAGES: _____
_____
_____

RATINGS:
	1	2	3	4	5
CLEANLINESS	☆	☆	☆	☆	☆
AMBIENCE	☆	☆	☆	☆	☆
AMENITIES	☆	☆	☆	☆	☆
SOUND PROOFING	☆	☆	☆	☆	☆
QUALITY OF THE FLUSH	☆	☆	☆	☆	☆
TOILET PAPER	☆	☆	☆	☆	☆

OVERALL EXPERIENCE:
☐ BEST SEAT IN THE HOUSE   ★ ★ ★ ★ ★
☐ WOULD POOP HERE AGAIN   ★ ★ ★ ★
☐ SHIT GOT REAL   ★ ★ ★
☐ SAME SHIT DIFFERENT HOUSE   ★ ★
☐ THINGS JUST DIDN'T COME OUT RIGHT   ★

Welcome! PLEASE SEAT YOURSELF AND ENJOY YOUR VISIT!

NAME: _____ DATE: _____ TIME: _____ DURATION OF VISIT: _____
HRS   MIN   SEC

PURPOSE FOR VISIT: ▢ #1 ▢ #2 ▢ OTHER: _____ SUCCESS? ▢ YES ▢ NO

FAVORITE EUPHEMISM FOR PERFORMING #1:

FAVORITE EUPHEMISM FOR PERFORMING #2:

FAVORITE RESTROOM GRAFFITI OR YOUR ORIGNAL DOODLE:

WHILE YOU WERE HERE, DID YOU:
☐ TEXT SOMEONE
☐ MAKE A PHONE CALL
☐ EMAIL
☐ CHECK SOCIAL MEDIA
☐ TAKE A SELFIE
☐ LOOK IN THE MEDICINE CABINET
☐ CHECK YOUR TEETH
☐ CHECK OUT YOUR BUTT
☐ CHECK YOUR FLY
☐ READ
☐ FIX YOUR HAIR
☐ TAKE SOME EXTRA "ME TIME"
☐ TALK TO YOURSELF
☐ CONDUCT BUSINESS OTHER THAN YOUR "BUSINESS." CARE TO SHARE?
_____

FAVORITE NAME FOR THIS ROOM:
☐ BATHROOM   ☐ JOHN
☐ TOILET   ☐ CAN
☐ POWDER ROOM   ☐ HEAD
☐ LAVATORY   ☐ POTTY
☐ SHITTER   ☐ CRAPPER
☐ LOO   ☐ WC
☐ LITTLE GIRLS ROOM
☐ LITTLE BOYS ROOM
☐ COMFORT STATION
☐ OTHER: _____
_____

RATINGS:
	1	2	3	4	5
CLEANLINESS	☆	☆	☆	☆	☆
AMBIENCE	☆	☆	☆	☆	☆
AMENITIES	☆	☆	☆	☆	☆
SOUND PROOFING	☆	☆	☆	☆	☆
QUALITY OF THE FLUSH	☆	☆	☆	☆	☆
TOILET PAPER	☆	☆	☆	☆	☆

OVERALL EXPERIENCE:
☐ BEST SEAT IN THE HOUSE ★★★★★
☐ WOULD POOP HERE AGAIN ★★★★
☐ SHIT GOT REAL ★★★
☐ SAME SHIT DIFFERENT HOUSE ★★
☐ THINGS JUST DIDN'T COME OUT RIGHT ★

THOUGHTS/MESSAGES: _____
_____
_____

Welcome! PLEASE SEAT YOURSELF AND ENJOY YOUR VISIT!

NAME: _____ DATE: _____ TIME: _____ DURATION OF VISIT: _____

HRS   MIN   SEC

PURPOSE FOR VISIT: 🧻 #1 🧻 #2 🧻 OTHER: _____   SUCCESS? 🧻 YES 🧻 NO

FAVORITE EUPHEMISM FOR PERFORMING #1:

FAVORITE RESTROOM GRAFFITI OR YOUR ORIGNAL DOODLE:

FAVORITE EUPHEMISM FOR PERFORMING #2:

WHILE YOU WERE HERE, DID YOU:
- ☐ TEXT SOMEONE
- ☐ MAKE A PHONE CALL
- ☐ EMAIL
- ☐ CHECK SOCIAL MEDIA
- ☐ TAKE A SELFIE
- ☐ LOOK IN THE MEDICINE CABINET
- ☐ CHECK YOUR TEETH
- ☐ CHECK OUT YOUR BUTT
- ☐ CHECK YOUR FLY
- ☐ READ
- ☐ FIX YOUR HAIR
- ☐ TAKE SOME EXTRA "ME TIME"
- ☐ TALK TO YOURSELF
- ☐ CONDUCT BUSINESS OTHER THAN YOUR "BUSINESS." CARE TO SHARE?
  _____

FAVORITE NAME FOR THIS ROOM:
- ☐ BATHROOM
- ☐ TOILET
- ☐ POWDER ROOM
- ☐ LAVATORY
- ☐ SHITTER
- ☐ LOO
- ☐ LITTLE GIRLS ROOM
- ☐ LITTLE BOYS ROOM
- ☐ COMFORT STATION
- ☐ OTHER: _____
- ☐ JOHN
- ☐ CAN
- ☐ HEAD
- ☐ POTTY
- ☐ CRAPPER
- ☐ WC

_____
_____

RATINGS:

	1	2	3	4	5
CLEANLINESS	☆	☆	☆	☆	☆
AMBIENCE	☆	☆	☆	☆	☆
AMENITIES	☆	☆	☆	☆	☆
SOUND PROOFING	☆	☆	☆	☆	☆
QUALITY OF THE FLUSH	☆	☆	☆	☆	☆
TOILET PAPER	☆	☆	☆	☆	☆

OVERALL EXPERIENCE:
- ☐ BEST SEAT IN THE HOUSE ★ ★ ★ ★ ★
- ☐ WOULD POOP HERE AGAIN ★ ★ ★ ★
- ☐ SHIT GOT REAL ★ ★ ★
- ☐ SAME SHIT DIFFERENT HOUSE ★ ★
- ☐ THINGS JUST DIDN'T COME OUT RIGHT ★

THOUGHTS/MESSAGES: _____
_____
_____

Welcome! PLEASE SEAT YOURSELF AND ENJOY YOUR VISIT!

NAME: _____ DATE: _____ TIME: _____ DURATION OF VISIT: _____
HRS   MIN   SEC

PURPOSE FOR VISIT: 🧻 #1 🧻 #2 🧻 OTHER: _____ SUCCESS? 🧻 YES 🧻 NO

FAVORITE EUPHEMISM FOR PERFORMING #1:

FAVORITE RESTROOM GRAFFITI OR YOUR ORIGNAL DOODLE:

FAVORITE EUPHEMISM FOR PERFORMING #2:

WHILE YOU WERE HERE, DID YOU:
- ☐ TEXT SOMEONE
- ☐ MAKE A PHONE CALL
- ☐ EMAIL
- ☐ CHECK SOCIAL MEDIA
- ☐ TAKE A SELFIE
- ☐ LOOK IN THE MEDICINE CABINET
- ☐ CHECK YOUR TEETH
- ☐ CHECK OUT YOUR BUTT
- ☐ CHECK YOUR FLY
- ☐ READ
- ☐ FIX YOUR HAIR
- ☐ TAKE SOME EXTRA "ME TIME"
- ☐ TALK TO YOURSELF
- ☐ CONDUCT BUSINESS OTHER THAN YOUR "BUSINESS." CARE TO SHARE?
_____

FAVORITE NAME FOR THIS ROOM:
- ☐ BATHROOM
- ☐ TOILET
- ☐ POWDER ROOM
- ☐ LAVATORY
- ☐ SHITTER
- ☐ LOO
- ☐ LITTLE GIRLS ROOM
- ☐ LITTLE BOYS ROOM
- ☐ COMFORT STATION
- ☐ OTHER: _____
- ☐ JOHN
- ☐ CAN
- ☐ HEAD
- ☐ POTTY
- ☐ CRAPPER
- ☐ WC

THOUGHTS/MESSAGES: _____
_____

RATINGS:
	1	2	3	4	5
CLEANLINESS	☆	☆	☆	☆	☆
AMBIENCE	☆	☆	☆	☆	☆
AMENITIES	☆	☆	☆	☆	☆
SOUND PROOFING	☆	☆	☆	☆	☆
QUALITY OF THE FLUSH	☆	☆	☆	☆	☆
TOILET PAPER	☆	☆	☆	☆	☆

OVERALL EXPERIENCE:
- ☐ BEST SEAT IN THE HOUSE ★ ★ ★ ★ ★
- ☐ WOULD POOP HERE AGAIN ★ ★ ★ ★
- ☐ SHIT GOT REAL ★ ★ ★
- ☐ SAME SHIT DIFFERENT HOUSE ★ ★
- ☐ THINGS JUST DIDN'T COME OUT RIGHT ★

Welcome! PLEASE SEAT YOURSELF AND ENJOY YOUR VISIT!

NAME: _____ DATE: _____ TIME: _____ DURATION OF VISIT: _____

HRS   MIN   SEC

PURPOSE FOR VISIT: ☐ #1 ☐ #2 ☐ OTHER: _____ SUCCESS? ☐ YES ☐ NO

FAVORITE EUPHEMISM FOR PERFORMING #1:

FAVORITE RESTROOM GRAFFITI OR YOUR ORIGNAL DOODLE:

FAVORITE EUPHEMISM FOR PERFORMING #2:

WHILE YOU WERE HERE, DID YOU:
- ☐ TEXT SOMEONE
- ☐ MAKE A PHONE CALL
- ☐ EMAIL
- ☐ CHECK SOCIAL MEDIA
- ☐ TAKE A SELFIE
- ☐ LOOK IN THE MEDICINE CABINET
- ☐ CHECK YOUR TEETH
- ☐ CHECK OUT YOUR BUTT
- ☐ CHECK YOUR FLY
- ☐ READ
- ☐ FIX YOUR HAIR
- ☐ TAKE SOME EXTRA "ME TIME"
- ☐ TALK TO YOURSELF
- ☐ CONDUCT BUSINESS OTHER THAN YOUR "BUSINESS." CARE TO SHARE?
  _____

FAVORITE NAME FOR THIS ROOM:
- ☐ BATHROOM
- ☐ TOILET
- ☐ POWDER ROOM
- ☐ LAVATORY
- ☐ SHITTER
- ☐ LOO
- ☐ JOHN
- ☐ CAN
- ☐ HEAD
- ☐ POTTY
- ☐ CRAPPER
- ☐ WC
- ☐ LITTLE GIRLS ROOM
- ☐ LITTLE BOYS ROOM
- ☐ COMFORT STATION
- ☐ OTHER: _____
  _____

THOUGHTS/MESSAGES: _____
_____
_____

RATINGS:
	1	2	3	4	5
CLEANLINESS	☆	☆	☆	☆	☆
AMBIENCE	☆	☆	☆	☆	☆
AMENITIES	☆	☆	☆	☆	☆
SOUND PROOFING	☆	☆	☆	☆	☆
QUALITY OF THE FLUSH	☆	☆	☆	☆	☆
TOILET PAPER	☆	☆	☆	☆	☆

OVERALL EXPERIENCE:
- ☐ BEST SEAT IN THE HOUSE ★ ★ ★ ★ ★
- ☐ WOULD POOP HERE AGAIN ★ ★ ★ ★
- ☐ SHIT GOT REAL ★ ★ ★
- ☐ SAME SHIT DIFFERENT HOUSE ★ ★
- ☐ THINGS JUST DIDN'T COME OUT RIGHT ★

Welcome! PLEASE SEAT YOURSELF AND ENJOY YOUR VISIT!

NAME: _____ DATE: _____ TIME: _____ DURATION OF VISIT: _____
HRS   MIN   SEC

PURPOSE FOR VISIT: ☐ #1 ☐ #2 ☐ OTHER: _____ SUCCESS? ☐ YES ☐ NO

FAVORITE EUPHEMISM FOR PERFORMING #1:

FAVORITE RESTROOM GRAFFITI OR YOUR ORIGNAL DOODLE:

FAVORITE EUPHEMISM FOR PERFORMING #2:

WHILE YOU WERE HERE, DID YOU:
☐ TEXT SOMEONE
☐ MAKE A PHONE CALL
☐ EMAIL
☐ CHECK SOCIAL MEDIA
☐ TAKE A SELFIE
☐ LOOK IN THE MEDICINE CABINET
☐ CHECK YOUR TEETH
☐ CHECK OUT YOUR BUTT
☐ CHECK YOUR FLY
☐ READ
☐ FIX YOUR HAIR
☐ TAKE SOME EXTRA "ME TIME"
☐ TALK TO YOURSELF
☐ CONDUCT BUSINESS OTHER THAN YOUR "BUSINESS." CARE TO SHARE?
_____

FAVORITE NAME FOR THIS ROOM:
☐ BATHROOM
☐ TOILET
☐ POWDER ROOM
☐ LAVATORY
☐ SHITTER
☐ LOO
☐ LITTLE GIRLS ROOM
☐ LITTLE BOYS ROOM
☐ COMFORT STATION
☐ OTHER: _____

☐ JOHN
☐ CAN
☐ HEAD
☐ POTTY
☐ CRAPPER
☐ WC

RATINGS: 1 2 3 4 5
CLEANLINESS   ☆ ☆ ☆ ☆ ☆
AMBIENCE   ☆ ☆ ☆ ☆ ☆
AMENITIES   ☆ ☆ ☆ ☆ ☆
SOUND PROOFING   ☆ ☆ ☆ ☆ ☆
QUALITY OF THE FLUSH ☆ ☆ ☆ ☆ ☆
TOILET PAPER   ☆ ☆ ☆ ☆ ☆

OVERALL EXPERIENCE:
☐ BEST SEAT IN THE HOUSE   ★ ★ ★ ★ ★
☐ WOULD POOP HERE AGAIN   ★ ★ ★ ★
☐ SHIT GOT REAL   ★ ★ ★
☐ SAME SHIT DIFFERENT HOUSE   ★ ★
☐ THINGS JUST DIDN'T COME OUT RIGHT   ★

THOUGHTS/MESSAGES: _____
_____

Welcome! PLEASE SEAT YOURSELF AND ENJOY YOUR VISIT!

NAME: _____ DATE: _____ TIME: _____ DURATION OF VISIT: _____
HRS   MIN   SEC

PURPOSE FOR VISIT: ☐ #1 ☐ #2 ☐ OTHER: _____ SUCCESS? ☐ YES ☐ NO

FAVORITE EUPHEMISM FOR PERFORMING #1:

FAVORITE EUPHEMISM FOR PERFORMING #2:

FAVORITE RESTROOM GRAFFITI OR YOUR ORIGNAL DOODLE:

WHILE YOU WERE HERE, DID YOU:
- ☐ TEXT SOMEONE
- ☐ MAKE A PHONE CALL
- ☐ EMAIL
- ☐ CHECK SOCIAL MEDIA
- ☐ TAKE A SELFIE
- ☐ LOOK IN THE MEDICINE CABINET
- ☐ CHECK YOUR TEETH
- ☐ CHECK OUT YOUR BUTT
- ☐ CHECK YOUR FLY
- ☐ READ
- ☐ FIX YOUR HAIR
- ☐ TAKE SOME EXTRA "ME TIME"
- ☐ TALK TO YOURSELF
- ☐ CONDUCT BUSINESS OTHER THAN YOUR "BUSINESS." CARE TO SHARE?
  _____

FAVORITE NAME FOR THIS ROOM:
- ☐ BATHROOM
- ☐ TOILET
- ☐ POWDER ROOM
- ☐ LAVATORY
- ☐ SHITTER
- ☐ LOO
- ☐ JOHN
- ☐ CAN
- ☐ HEAD
- ☐ POTTY
- ☐ CRAPPER
- ☐ WC
- ☐ LITTLE GIRLS ROOM
- ☐ LITTLE BOYS ROOM
- ☐ COMFORT STATION
- ☐ OTHER: _____
  _____

THOUGHTS/MESSAGES: _____
_____
_____

RATINGS:

	1	2	3	4	5
CLEANLINESS	☆	☆	☆	☆	☆
AMBIENCE	☆	☆	☆	☆	☆
AMENITIES	☆	☆	☆	☆	☆
SOUND PROOFING	☆	☆	☆	☆	☆
QUALITY OF THE FLUSH	☆	☆	☆	☆	☆
TOILET PAPER	☆	☆	☆	☆	☆

OVERALL EXPERIENCE:
- ☐ BEST SEAT IN THE HOUSE ★ ★ ★ ★ ★
- ☐ WOULD POOP HERE AGAIN ★ ★ ★ ★
- ☐ SHIT GOT REAL ★ ★ ★
- ☐ SAME SHIT DIFFERENT HOUSE ★ ★
- ☐ THINGS JUST DIDN'T COME OUT RIGHT ★

Welcome! PLEASE SEAT YOURSELF AND ENJOY YOUR VISIT!

NAME: _____ DATE: _____ TIME: _____ DURATION OF VISIT: _____
HRS   MIN   SEC

PURPOSE FOR VISIT: 🧻 #1 🧻 #2 🧻 OTHER: _____ SUCCESS? 🧻 YES 🧻 NO

FAVORITE EUPHEMISM FOR PERFORMING #1:

FAVORITE RESTROOM GRAFFITI OR YOUR ORIGNAL DOODLE:

FAVORITE EUPHEMISM FOR PERFORMING #2:

WHILE YOU WERE HERE, DID YOU:
- ☐ TEXT SOMEONE
- ☐ MAKE A PHONE CALL
- ☐ EMAIL
- ☐ CHECK SOCIAL MEDIA
- ☐ TAKE A SELFIE
- ☐ LOOK IN THE MEDICINE CABINET
- ☐ CHECK YOUR TEETH
- ☐ CHECK OUT YOUR BUTT
- ☐ CHECK YOUR FLY
- ☐ READ
- ☐ FIX YOUR HAIR
- ☐ TAKE SOME EXTRA "ME TIME"
- ☐ TALK TO YOURSELF
- ☐ CONDUCT BUSINESS OTHER THAN YOUR "BUSINESS." CARE TO SHARE?
_____

FAVORITE NAME FOR THIS ROOM:
- ☐ BATHROOM
- ☐ TOILET
- ☐ POWDER ROOM
- ☐ LAVATORY
- ☐ SHITTER
- ☐ LOO
- ☐ LITTLE GIRLS ROOM
- ☐ LITTLE BOYS ROOM
- ☐ COMFORT STATION
- ☐ JOHN
- ☐ CAN
- ☐ HEAD
- ☐ POTTY
- ☐ CRAPPER
- ☐ WC
- ☐ OTHER: _____
_____

RATINGS:
	1	2	3	4	5
CLEANLINESS	☆	☆	☆	☆	☆
AMBIENCE	☆	☆	☆	☆	☆
AMENITIES	☆	☆	☆	☆	☆
SOUND PROOFING	☆	☆	☆	☆	☆
QUALITY OF THE FLUSH	☆	☆	☆	☆	☆
TOILET PAPER	☆	☆	☆	☆	☆

OVERALL EXPERIENCE:
- ☐ BEST SEAT IN THE HOUSE ★ ★ ★ ★ ★
- ☐ WOULD POOP HERE AGAIN ★ ★ ★ ★
- ☐ SHIT GOT REAL ★ ★ ★
- ☐ SAME SHIT DIFFERENT HOUSE ★ ★
- ☐ THINGS JUST DIDN'T COME OUT RIGHT ★

THOUGHTS/MESSAGES: _____
_____
_____

Welcome! PLEASE SEAT YOURSELF AND ENJOY YOUR VISIT!

NAME: _____ DATE: _____ TIME: _____ DURATION OF VISIT: _____

HRS   MIN   SEC

PURPOSE FOR VISIT: ☐ #1 ☐ #2 ☐ OTHER: _____ SUCCESS? ☐ YES ☐ NO

FAVORITE EUPHEMISM FOR PERFORMING #1:

FAVORITE RESTROOM GRAFFITI OR YOUR ORIGNAL DOODLE:

FAVORITE EUPHEMISM FOR PERFORMING #2:

WHILE YOU WERE HERE, DID YOU:
- ☐ TEXT SOMEONE
- ☐ MAKE A PHONE CALL
- ☐ EMAIL
- ☐ CHECK SOCIAL MEDIA
- ☐ TAKE A SELFIE
- ☐ LOOK IN THE MEDICINE CABINET
- ☐ CHECK YOUR TEETH
- ☐ CHECK OUT YOUR BUTT
- ☐ CHECK YOUR FLY
- ☐ READ
- ☐ FIX YOUR HAIR
- ☐ TAKE SOME EXTRA "ME TIME"
- ☐ TALK TO YOURSELF
- ☐ CONDUCT BUSINESS OTHER THAN YOUR "BUSINESS." CARE TO SHARE?

FAVORITE NAME FOR THIS ROOM:
- ☐ BATHROOM
- ☐ TOILET
- ☐ POWDER ROOM
- ☐ LAVATORY
- ☐ SHITTER
- ☐ LOO
- ☐ LITTLE GIRLS ROOM
- ☐ LITTLE BOYS ROOM
- ☐ COMFORT STATION
- ☐ OTHER: _____
- ☐ JOHN
- ☐ CAN
- ☐ HEAD
- ☐ POTTY
- ☐ CRAPPER
- ☐ WC

RATINGS:
	1	2	3	4	5
CLEANLINESS	☆	☆	☆	☆	☆
AMBIENCE	☆	☆	☆	☆	☆
AMENITIES	☆	☆	☆	☆	☆
SOUND PROOFING	☆	☆	☆	☆	☆
QUALITY OF THE FLUSH	☆	☆	☆	☆	☆
TOILET PAPER	☆	☆	☆	☆	☆

OVERALL EXPERIENCE:
- ☐ BEST SEAT IN THE HOUSE ★ ★ ★ ★ ★
- ☐ WOULD POOP HERE AGAIN ★ ★ ★ ★
- ☐ SHIT GOT REAL ★ ★ ★
- ☐ SAME SHIT DIFFERENT HOUSE ★ ★
- ☐ THINGS JUST DIDN'T COME OUT RIGHT ★

THOUGHTS/MESSAGES: _____
_____
_____

Welcome! PLEASE SEAT YOURSELF AND ENJOY YOUR VISIT!

NAME: _____ DATE: _____ TIME: _____ DURATION OF VISIT: _____
HRS   MIN   SEC

PURPOSE FOR VISIT: 🧻 #1 🧻 #2 🧻 OTHER: _____ SUCCESS? 🧻 YES 🧻 NO

FAVORITE EUPHEMISM FOR PERFORMING #1:

FAVORITE EUPHEMISM FOR PERFORMING #2:

FAVORITE RESTROOM GRAFFITI OR YOUR ORIGNAL DOODLE:

WHILE YOU WERE HERE, DID YOU:
- ☐ TEXT SOMEONE
- ☐ MAKE A PHONE CALL
- ☐ EMAIL
- ☐ CHECK SOCIAL MEDIA
- ☐ TAKE A SELFIE
- ☐ LOOK IN THE MEDICINE CABINET
- ☐ CHECK YOUR TEETH
- ☐ CHECK OUT YOUR BUTT
- ☐ CHECK YOUR FLY
- ☐ READ
- ☐ FIX YOUR HAIR
- ☐ TAKE SOME EXTRA "ME TIME"
- ☐ TALK TO YOURSELF
- ☐ CONDUCT BUSINESS OTHER THAN YOUR "BUSINESS." CARE TO SHARE?
  _____

FAVORITE NAME FOR THIS ROOM:
- ☐ BATHROOM
- ☐ TOILET
- ☐ POWDER ROOM
- ☐ LAVATORY
- ☐ SHITTER
- ☐ LOO
- ☐ LITTLE GIRLS ROOM
- ☐ LITTLE BOYS ROOM
- ☐ COMFORT STATION
- ☐ OTHER: _____
- ☐ JOHN
- ☐ CAN
- ☐ HEAD
- ☐ POTTY
- ☐ CRAPPER
- ☐ WC

RATINGS:

	1	2	3	4	5
CLEANLINESS	☆	☆	☆	☆	☆
AMBIENCE	☆	☆	☆	☆	☆
AMENITIES	☆	☆	☆	☆	☆
SOUND PROOFING	☆	☆	☆	☆	☆
QUALITY OF THE FLUSH	☆	☆	☆	☆	☆
TOILET PAPER	☆	☆	☆	☆	☆

OVERALL EXPERIENCE:
- ☐ BEST SEAT IN THE HOUSE ★ ★ ★ ★ ★
- ☐ WOULD POOP HERE AGAIN ★ ★ ★ ★
- ☐ SHIT GOT REAL ★ ★ ★
- ☐ SAME SHIT DIFFERENT HOUSE ★ ★
- ☐ THINGS JUST DIDN'T COME OUT RIGHT ★

THOUGHTS/MESSAGES: _____
_____

Welcome! PLEASE SEAT YOURSELF AND ENJOY YOUR VISIT!

NAME: _____ DATE: _____ TIME: _____ DURATION OF VISIT: _____
HRS   MIN   SEC

PURPOSE FOR VISIT: 🧻 #1 🧻 #2 🧻 OTHER: _____ SUCCESS? 🧻 YES 🧻 NO

FAVORITE EUPHEMISM FOR PERFORMING #1:

FAVORITE RESTROOM GRAFFITI OR YOUR ORIGNAL DOODLE:

FAVORITE EUPHEMISM FOR PERFORMING #2:

WHILE YOU WERE HERE, DID YOU:
- ☐ TEXT SOMEONE
- ☐ MAKE A PHONE CALL
- ☐ EMAIL
- ☐ CHECK SOCIAL MEDIA
- ☐ TAKE A SELFIE
- ☐ LOOK IN THE MEDICINE CABINET
- ☐ CHECK YOUR TEETH
- ☐ CHECK OUT YOUR BUTT
- ☐ CHECK YOUR FLY
- ☐ READ
- ☐ FIX YOUR HAIR
- ☐ TAKE SOME EXTRA "ME TIME"
- ☐ TALK TO YOURSELF
- ☐ CONDUCT BUSINESS OTHER THAN YOUR "BUSINESS." CARE TO SHARE?
  _____

FAVORITE NAME FOR THIS ROOM:
- ☐ BATHROOM
- ☐ TOILET
- ☐ POWDER ROOM
- ☐ LAVATORY
- ☐ SHITTER
- ☐ LOO
- ☐ LITTLE GIRLS ROOM
- ☐ LITTLE BOYS ROOM
- ☐ COMFORT STATION
- ☐ OTHER: _____
- ☐ JOHN
- ☐ CAN
- ☐ HEAD
- ☐ POTTY
- ☐ CRAPPER
- ☐ WC

THOUGHTS/MESSAGES: _____

RATINGS:

	1	2	3	4	5
CLEANLINESS	☆	☆	☆	☆	☆
AMBIENCE	☆	☆	☆	☆	☆
AMENITIES	☆	☆	☆	☆	☆
SOUND PROOFING	☆	☆	☆	☆	☆
QUALITY OF THE FLUSH	☆	☆	☆	☆	☆
TOILET PAPER	☆	☆	☆	☆	☆

OVERALL EXPERIENCE:
- ☐ BEST SEAT IN THE HOUSE ★ ★ ★ ★ ★
- ☐ WOULD POOP HERE AGAIN ★ ★ ★ ★
- ☐ SHIT GOT REAL ★ ★ ★
- ☐ SAME SHIT DIFFERENT HOUSE ★ ★
- ☐ THINGS JUST DIDN'T COME OUT RIGHT ★

Welcome! PLEASE SEAT YOURSELF AND ENJOY YOUR VISIT!

NAME: _____ DATE: _____ TIME: _____ DURATION OF VISIT: _____
HRS   MIN   SEC

PURPOSE FOR VISIT: 🧻 #1 🧻 #2 🧻 OTHER: _____ SUCCESS? 🧻 YES 🧻 NO

FAVORITE EUPHEMISM FOR PERFORMING #1:

FAVORITE EUPHEMISM FOR PERFORMING #2:

FAVORITE RESTROOM GRAFFITI OR YOUR ORIGNAL DOODLE:

WHILE YOU WERE HERE, DID YOU:
- ☐ TEXT SOMEONE
- ☐ MAKE A PHONE CALL
- ☐ EMAIL
- ☐ CHECK SOCIAL MEDIA
- ☐ TAKE A SELFIE
- ☐ LOOK IN THE MEDICINE CABINET
- ☐ CHECK YOUR TEETH
- ☐ CHECK OUT YOUR BUTT
- ☐ CHECK YOUR FLY
- ☐ READ
- ☐ FIX YOUR HAIR
- ☐ TAKE SOME EXTRA "ME TIME"
- ☐ TALK TO YOURSELF
- ☐ CONDUCT BUSINESS OTHER THAN YOUR "BUSINESS." CARE TO SHARE?
  _____

FAVORITE NAME FOR THIS ROOM:
- ☐ BATHROOM
- ☐ TOILET
- ☐ POWDER ROOM
- ☐ LAVATORY
- ☐ SHITTER
- ☐ LOO
- ☐ LITTLE GIRLS ROOM
- ☐ LITTLE BOYS ROOM
- ☐ COMFORT STATION
- ☐ OTHER: _____
- ☐ JOHN
- ☐ CAN
- ☐ HEAD
- ☐ POTTY
- ☐ CRAPPER
- ☐ WC

_____

RATINGS:
	1	2	3	4	5
CLEANLINESS	☆	☆	☆	☆	☆
AMBIENCE	☆	☆	☆	☆	☆
AMENITIES	☆	☆	☆	☆	☆
SOUND PROOFING	☆	☆	☆	☆	☆
QUALITY OF THE FLUSH	☆	☆	☆	☆	☆
TOILET PAPER	☆	☆	☆	☆	☆

OVERALL EXPERIENCE:
- ☐ BEST SEAT IN THE HOUSE ★★★★★
- ☐ WOULD POOP HERE AGAIN ★★★★
- ☐ SHIT GOT REAL ★★★
- ☐ SAME SHIT DIFFERENT HOUSE ★★
- ☐ THINGS JUST DIDN'T COME OUT RIGHT ★

THOUGHTS/MESSAGES: _____
_____
_____

Welcome! PLEASE SEAT YOURSELF AND ENJOY YOUR VISIT!

NAME: _____ DATE: _____ TIME: _____ DURATION OF VISIT: _____
                                                                              HRS   MIN   SEC

PURPOSE FOR VISIT: ☐ #1 ☐ #2 ☐ OTHER: _____ SUCCESS? ☐ YES ☐ NO

FAVORITE EUPHEMISM FOR PERFORMING #1: _____

FAVORITE RESTROOM GRAFFITI OR YOUR ORIGNAL DOODLE:

FAVORITE EUPHEMISM FOR PERFORMING #2: _____

WHILE YOU WERE HERE, DID YOU:
- ☐ TEXT SOMEONE
- ☐ MAKE A PHONE CALL
- ☐ EMAIL
- ☐ CHECK SOCIAL MEDIA
- ☐ TAKE A SELFIE
- ☐ LOOK IN THE MEDICINE CABINET
- ☐ CHECK YOUR TEETH
- ☐ CHECK OUT YOUR BUTT
- ☐ CHECK YOUR FLY
- ☐ READ
- ☐ FIX YOUR HAIR
- ☐ TAKE SOME EXTRA "ME TIME"
- ☐ TALK TO YOURSELF
- ☐ CONDUCT BUSINESS OTHER THAN YOUR "BUSINESS." CARE TO SHARE?
_____

FAVORITE NAME FOR THIS ROOM:
- ☐ BATHROOM
- ☐ TOILET
- ☐ POWDER ROOM
- ☐ LAVATORY
- ☐ SHITTER
- ☐ LOO
- ☐ LITTLE GIRLS ROOM
- ☐ LITTLE BOYS ROOM
- ☐ COMFORT STATION
- ☐ OTHER: _____
- ☐ JOHN
- ☐ CAN
- ☐ HEAD
- ☐ POTTY
- ☐ CRAPPER
- ☐ WC

_____

THOUGHTS/MESSAGES: _____

RATINGS:

	1	2	3	4	5
CLEANLINESS	☆	☆	☆	☆	☆
AMBIENCE	☆	☆	☆	☆	☆
AMENITIES	☆	☆	☆	☆	☆
SOUND PROOFING	☆	☆	☆	☆	☆
QUALITY OF THE FLUSH	☆	☆	☆	☆	☆
TOILET PAPER	☆	☆	☆	☆	☆

OVERALL EXPERIENCE:
- ☐ BEST SEAT IN THE HOUSE ★ ★ ★ ★ ★
- ☐ WOULD POOP HERE AGAIN ★ ★ ★ ★
- ☐ SHIT GOT REAL ★ ★ ★
- ☐ SAME SHIT DIFFERENT HOUSE ★ ★
- ☐ THINGS JUST DIDN'T COME OUT RIGHT ★

Welcome! PLEASE SEAT YOURSELF AND ENJOY YOUR VISIT!

NAME: _____ DATE: _____ TIME: _____ DURATION OF VISIT: _____
HRS   MIN   SEC

PURPOSE FOR VISIT: 🧻 #1 🧻 #2 🧻 OTHER: _____ SUCCESS? 🧻 YES 🧻 NO

FAVORITE EUPHEMISM FOR PERFORMING #1:

FAVORITE RESTROOM GRAFFITI OR YOUR ORIGNAL DOODLE:

FAVORITE EUPHEMISM FOR PERFORMING #2:

WHILE YOU WERE HERE, DID YOU:
- ☐ TEXT SOMEONE
- ☐ MAKE A PHONE CALL
- ☐ EMAIL
- ☐ CHECK SOCIAL MEDIA
- ☐ TAKE A SELFIE
- ☐ LOOK IN THE MEDICINE CABINET
- ☐ CHECK YOUR TEETH
- ☐ CHECK OUT YOUR BUTT
- ☐ CHECK YOUR FLY
- ☐ READ
- ☐ FIX YOUR HAIR
- ☐ TAKE SOME EXTRA "ME TIME"
- ☐ TALK TO YOURSELF
- ☐ CONDUCT BUSINESS OTHER THAN YOUR "BUSINESS." CARE TO SHARE?
_____

FAVORITE NAME FOR THIS ROOM:
- ☐ BATHROOM
- ☐ TOILET
- ☐ POWDER ROOM
- ☐ LAVATORY
- ☐ SHITTER
- ☐ LOO
- ☐ LITTLE GIRLS ROOM
- ☐ LITTLE BOYS ROOM
- ☐ COMFORT STATION
- ☐ OTHER: _____
- ☐ JOHN
- ☐ CAN
- ☐ HEAD
- ☐ POTTY
- ☐ CRAPPER
- ☐ WC
_____

THOUGHTS/MESSAGES: _____
_____
_____

RATINGS: 1 2 3 4 5
CLEANLINESS   ☆ ☆ ☆ ☆ ☆
AMBIENCE   ☆ ☆ ☆ ☆ ☆
AMENITIES   ☆ ☆ ☆ ☆ ☆
SOUND PROOFING   ☆ ☆ ☆ ☆ ☆
QUALITY OF THE FLUSH   ☆ ☆ ☆ ☆ ☆
TOILET PAPER   ☆ ☆ ☆ ☆ ☆

OVERALL EXPERIENCE:
- ☐ BEST SEAT IN THE HOUSE   ★ ★ ★ ★ ★
- ☐ WOULD POOP HERE AGAIN   ★ ★ ★ ★
- ☐ SHIT GOT REAL   ★ ★ ★
- ☐ SAME SHIT DIFFERENT HOUSE   ★ ★
- ☐ THINGS JUST DIDN'T COME OUT RIGHT ★

Welcome! PLEASE SEAT YOURSELF AND ENJOY YOUR VISIT!

NAME: _____ DATE: _____ TIME: _____ DURATION OF VISIT: _____

HRS   MIN   SEC

PURPOSE FOR VISIT: ☐ #1 ☐ #2 ☐ OTHER: _____   SUCCESS? ☐ YES ☐ NO

FAVORITE EUPHEMISM FOR PERFORMING #1:

FAVORITE RESTROOM GRAFFITI OR YOUR ORIGNAL DOODLE:

FAVORITE EUPHEMISM FOR PERFORMING #2:

WHILE YOU WERE HERE, DID YOU:
- ☐ TEXT SOMEONE
- ☐ MAKE A PHONE CALL
- ☐ EMAIL
- ☐ CHECK SOCIAL MEDIA
- ☐ TAKE A SELFIE
- ☐ LOOK IN THE MEDICINE CABINET
- ☐ CHECK YOUR TEETH
- ☐ CHECK OUT YOUR BUTT
- ☐ CHECK YOUR FLY
- ☐ READ
- ☐ FIX YOUR HAIR
- ☐ TAKE SOME EXTRA "ME TIME"
- ☐ TALK TO YOURSELF
- ☐ CONDUCT BUSINESS OTHER THAN YOUR "BUSINESS." CARE TO SHARE?
_____

FAVORITE NAME FOR THIS ROOM:
- ☐ BATHROOM
- ☐ TOILET
- ☐ POWDER ROOM
- ☐ LAVATORY
- ☐ SHITTER
- ☐ LOO
- ☐ LITTLE GIRLS ROOM
- ☐ LITTLE BOYS ROOM
- ☐ COMFORT STATION
- ☐ OTHER: _____

- ☐ JOHN
- ☐ CAN
- ☐ HEAD
- ☐ POTTY
- ☐ CRAPPER
- ☐ WC

THOUGHTS/MESSAGES: _____
_____
_____

RATINGS:

	1	2	3	4	5
CLEANLINESS	☆	☆	☆	☆	☆
AMBIENCE	☆	☆	☆	☆	☆
AMENITIES	☆	☆	☆	☆	☆
SOUND PROOFING	☆	☆	☆	☆	☆
QUALITY OF THE FLUSH	☆	☆	☆	☆	☆
TOILET PAPER	☆	☆	☆	☆	☆

OVERALL EXPERIENCE:
- ☐ BEST SEAT IN THE HOUSE ★ ★ ★ ★ ★
- ☐ WOULD POOP HERE AGAIN ★ ★ ★ ★
- ☐ SHIT GOT REAL ★ ★ ★
- ☐ SAME SHIT DIFFERENT HOUSE ★ ★
- ☐ THINGS JUST DIDN'T COME OUT RIGHT ★

Welcome! PLEASE SEAT YOURSELF AND ENJOY YOUR VISIT!

NAME: _____ DATE: _____ TIME: _____ DURATION OF VISIT: _____
HRS   MIN   SEC

PURPOSE FOR VISIT: 🧻 #1   🧻 #2   🧻 OTHER: _____   SUCCESS? 🧻 YES   🧻 NO

FAVORITE EUPHEMISM FOR PERFORMING #1:

FAVORITE EUPHEMISM FOR PERFORMING #2:

FAVORITE RESTROOM GRAFFITI OR YOUR ORIGNAL DOODLE:

WHILE YOU WERE HERE, DID YOU:
- ☐ TEXT SOMEONE
- ☐ MAKE A PHONE CALL
- ☐ EMAIL
- ☐ CHECK SOCIAL MEDIA
- ☐ TAKE A SELFIE
- ☐ LOOK IN THE MEDICINE CABINET
- ☐ CHECK YOUR TEETH
- ☐ CHECK OUT YOUR BUTT
- ☐ CHECK YOUR FLY
- ☐ READ
- ☐ FIX YOUR HAIR
- ☐ TAKE SOME EXTRA "ME TIME"
- ☐ TALK TO YOURSELF
- ☐ CONDUCT BUSINESS OTHER THAN YOUR "BUSINESS." CARE TO SHARE?
_____

FAVORITE NAME FOR THIS ROOM:
- ☐ BATHROOM
- ☐ TOILET
- ☐ POWDER ROOM
- ☐ LAVATORY
- ☐ SHITTER
- ☐ LOO
- ☐ LITTLE GIRLS ROOM
- ☐ LITTLE BOYS ROOM
- ☐ COMFORT STATION
- ☐ OTHER: _____

- ☐ JOHN
- ☐ CAN
- ☐ HEAD
- ☐ POTTY
- ☐ CRAPPER
- ☐ WC

RATINGS:

	1	2	3	4	5
CLEANLINESS	☆	☆	☆	☆	☆
AMBIENCE	☆	☆	☆	☆	☆
AMENITIES	☆	☆	☆	☆	☆
SOUND PROOFING	☆	☆	☆	☆	☆
QUALITY OF THE FLUSH	☆	☆	☆	☆	☆
TOILET PAPER	☆	☆	☆	☆	☆

OVERALL EXPERIENCE:
- ☐ BEST SEAT IN THE HOUSE ★★★★★
- ☐ WOULD POOP HERE AGAIN ★★★★
- ☐ SHIT GOT REAL ★★★
- ☐ SAME SHIT DIFFERENT HOUSE ★★
- ☐ THINGS JUST DIDN'T COME OUT RIGHT ★

THOUGHTS/MESSAGES: _____
_____

 **Welcome!** PLEASE SEAT YOURSELF AND ENJOY YOUR VISIT!

NAME: _____ DATE: _____ TIME: _____ DURATION OF VISIT: _____
                                                                            HRS   MIN   SEC

PURPOSE FOR VISIT: 🧻 #1 🧻 #2 🧻 OTHER: _____ SUCCESS? 🧻 YES 🧻 NO

FAVORITE EUPHEMISM FOR PERFORMING #1:

FAVORITE EUPHEMISM FOR PERFORMING #2:

FAVORITE RESTROOM GRAFFITI OR YOUR ORIGNAL DOODLE:

WHILE YOU WERE HERE, DID YOU:
☐ TEXT SOMEONE
☐ MAKE A PHONE CALL
☐ EMAIL
☐ CHECK SOCIAL MEDIA
☐ TAKE A SELFIE
☐ LOOK IN THE MEDICINE CABINET
☐ CHECK YOUR TEETH
☐ CHECK OUT YOUR BUTT
☐ CHECK YOUR FLY
☐ READ
☐ FIX YOUR HAIR
☐ TAKE SOME EXTRA "ME TIME"
☐ TALK TO YOURSELF
☐ CONDUCT BUSINESS OTHER THAN YOUR "BUSINESS." CARE TO SHARE?

FAVORITE NAME FOR THIS ROOM:
☐ BATHROOM   ☐ JOHN
☐ TOILET   ☐ CAN
☐ POWDER ROOM   ☐ HEAD
☐ LAVATORY   ☐ POTTY
☐ SHITTER   ☐ CRAPPER
☐ LOO   ☐ WC
☐ LITTLE GIRLS ROOM
☐ LITTLE BOYS ROOM
☐ COMFORT STATION
☐ OTHER: _____
_____

THOUGHTS/MESSAGES: _____
_____

RATINGS: 1 2 3 4 5
CLEANLINESS   ☆ ☆ ☆ ☆ ☆
AMBIENCE   ☆ ☆ ☆ ☆ ☆
AMENITIES   ☆ ☆ ☆ ☆ ☆
SOUND PROOFING   ☆ ☆ ☆ ☆ ☆
QUALITY OF THE FLUSH   ☆ ☆ ☆ ☆ ☆
TOILET PAPER   ☆ ☆ ☆ ☆ ☆

OVERALL EXPERIENCE:
☐ BEST SEAT IN THE HOUSE   ★ ★ ★ ★ ★
☐ WOULD POOP HERE AGAIN   ★ ★ ★ ★
☐ SHIT GOT REAL   ★ ★ ★
☐ SAME SHIT DIFFERENT HOUSE   ★ ★
☐ THINGS JUST DIDN'T COME OUT RIGHT ★

Welcome! PLEASE SEAT YOURSELF AND ENJOY YOUR VISIT!

NAME: _____ DATE: _____ TIME: _____ DURATION OF VISIT: _____
HRS   MIN   SEC

PURPOSE FOR VISIT: 🧻 #1 🧻 #2 🧻 OTHER: _____   SUCCESS? 🧻 YES 🧻 NO

FAVORITE EUPHEMISM FOR PERFORMING #1:   FAVORITE RESTROOM GRAFFITI OR YOUR ORIGNAL DOODLE:

FAVORITE EUPHEMISM FOR PERFORMING #2:

WHILE YOU WERE HERE, DID YOU:
- ☐ TEXT SOMEONE
- ☐ MAKE A PHONE CALL
- ☐ EMAIL
- ☐ CHECK SOCIAL MEDIA
- ☐ TAKE A SELFIE
- ☐ LOOK IN THE MEDICINE CABINET
- ☐ CHECK YOUR TEETH
- ☐ CHECK OUT YOUR BUTT
- ☐ CHECK YOUR FLY
- ☐ READ
- ☐ FIX YOUR HAIR
- ☐ TAKE SOME EXTRA "ME TIME"
- ☐ TALK TO YOURSELF
- ☐ CONDUCT BUSINESS OTHER THAN YOUR "BUSINESS." CARE TO SHARE?
_____

FAVORITE NAME FOR THIS ROOM:
- ☐ BATHROOM
- ☐ TOILET
- ☐ POWDER ROOM
- ☐ LAVATORY
- ☐ SHITTER
- ☐ LOO
- ☐ LITTLE GIRLS ROOM
- ☐ LITTLE BOYS ROOM
- ☐ COMFORT STATION
- ☐ OTHER: _____

- ☐ JOHN
- ☐ CAN
- ☐ HEAD
- ☐ POTTY
- ☐ CRAPPER
- ☐ WC

RATINGS: 1 2 3 4 5
CLEANLINESS   ☆ ☆ ☆ ☆ ☆
AMBIENCE   ☆ ☆ ☆ ☆ ☆
AMENITIES   ☆ ☆ ☆ ☆ ☆
SOUND PROOFING   ☆ ☆ ☆ ☆ ☆
QUALITY OF THE FLUSH   ☆ ☆ ☆ ☆ ☆
TOILET PAPER   ☆ ☆ ☆ ☆ ☆

OVERALL EXPERIENCE:
- ☐ BEST SEAT IN THE HOUSE   ★ ★ ★ ★ ★
- ☐ WOULD POOP HERE AGAIN   ★ ★ ★ ★
- ☐ SHIT GOT REAL   ★ ★ ★
- ☐ SAME SHIT DIFFERENT HOUSE   ★ ★
- ☐ THINGS JUST DIDN'T COME OUT RIGHT   ★

THOUGHTS/MESSAGES: _____
_____

Welcome! PLEASE SEAT YOURSELF AND ENJOY YOUR VISIT!

NAME: _____ DATE: _____ TIME: _____ DURATION OF VISIT: _____
HRS   MIN   SEC

PURPOSE FOR VISIT: ☐ #1 ☐ #2 ☐ OTHER: _____ SUCCESS? ☐ YES ☐ NO

FAVORITE EUPHEMISM FOR PERFORMING #1:

FAVORITE RESTROOM GRAFFITI OR YOUR ORIGNAL DOODLE:

FAVORITE EUPHEMISM FOR PERFORMING #2:

WHILE YOU WERE HERE, DID YOU:
☐ TEXT SOMEONE
☐ MAKE A PHONE CALL
☐ EMAIL
☐ CHECK SOCIAL MEDIA
☐ TAKE A SELFIE
☐ LOOK IN THE MEDICINE CABINET
☐ CHECK YOUR TEETH
☐ CHECK OUT YOUR BUTT
☐ CHECK YOUR FLY
☐ READ
☐ FIX YOUR HAIR
☐ TAKE SOME EXTRA "ME TIME"
☐ TALK TO YOURSELF
☐ CONDUCT BUSINESS OTHER THAN YOUR "BUSINESS." CARE TO SHARE?
_____

FAVORITE NAME FOR THIS ROOM:
☐ BATHROOM   ☐ JOHN
☐ TOILET   ☐ CAN
☐ POWDER ROOM   ☐ HEAD
☐ LAVATORY   ☐ POTTY
☐ SHITTER   ☐ CRAPPER
☐ LOO   ☐ WC
☐ LITTLE GIRLS ROOM
☐ LITTLE BOYS ROOM
☐ COMFORT STATION
☐ OTHER: _____
_____

THOUGHTS/MESSAGES: _____
_____
_____

RATINGS: 1 2 3 4 5
CLEANLINESS   ☆ ☆ ☆ ☆ ☆
AMBIENCE   ☆ ☆ ☆ ☆ ☆
AMENITIES   ☆ ☆ ☆ ☆ ☆
SOUND PROOFING   ☆ ☆ ☆ ☆ ☆
QUALITY OF THE FLUSH ☆ ☆ ☆ ☆ ☆
TOILET PAPER   ☆ ☆ ☆ ☆ ☆

OVERALL EXPERIENCE:
☐ BEST SEAT IN THE HOUSE   ★ ★ ★ ★ ★
☐ WOULD POOP HERE AGAIN   ★ ★ ★ ★
☐ SHIT GOT REAL   ★ ★ ★
☐ SAME SHIT DIFFERENT HOUSE   ★ ★
☐ THINGS JUST DIDN'T COME OUT RIGHT ★

Welcome! PLEASE SEAT YOURSELF AND ENJOY YOUR VISIT!

NAME: _____ DATE: _____ TIME: _____ DURATION OF VISIT: _____

HRS   MIN   SEC

PURPOSE FOR VISIT: 🧻 #1 🧻 #2 🧻 OTHER: _____ SUCCESS? 🧻 YES 🧻 NO

FAVORITE EUPHEMISM FOR PERFORMING #1:

FAVORITE RESTROOM GRAFFITI OR YOUR ORIGNAL DOODLE:

FAVORITE EUPHEMISM FOR PERFORMING #2:

WHILE YOU WERE HERE, DID YOU:
- ☐ TEXT SOMEONE
- ☐ MAKE A PHONE CALL
- ☐ EMAIL
- ☐ CHECK SOCIAL MEDIA
- ☐ TAKE A SELFIE
- ☐ LOOK IN THE MEDICINE CABINET
- ☐ CHECK YOUR TEETH
- ☐ CHECK OUT YOUR BUTT
- ☐ CHECK YOUR FLY
- ☐ READ
- ☐ FIX YOUR HAIR
- ☐ TAKE SOME EXTRA "ME TIME"
- ☐ TALK TO YOURSELF
- ☐ CONDUCT BUSINESS OTHER THAN YOUR "BUSINESS." CARE TO SHARE?
  _____

FAVORITE NAME FOR THIS ROOM:
- ☐ BATHROOM
- ☐ TOILET
- ☐ POWDER ROOM
- ☐ LAVATORY
- ☐ SHITTER
- ☐ LOO
- ☐ LITTLE GIRLS ROOM
- ☐ LITTLE BOYS ROOM
- ☐ COMFORT STATION
- ☐ OTHER: _____
- ☐ JOHN
- ☐ CAN
- ☐ HEAD
- ☐ POTTY
- ☐ CRAPPER
- ☐ WC

_____
_____

RATINGS:

	1	2	3	4	5
CLEANLINESS	☆	☆	☆	☆	☆
AMBIENCE	☆	☆	☆	☆	☆
AMENITIES	☆	☆	☆	☆	☆
SOUND PROOFING	☆	☆	☆	☆	☆
QUALITY OF THE FLUSH	☆	☆	☆	☆	☆
TOILET PAPER	☆	☆	☆	☆	☆

OVERALL EXPERIENCE:
- ☐ BEST SEAT IN THE HOUSE ★ ★ ★ ★ ★
- ☐ WOULD POOP HERE AGAIN ★ ★ ★ ★
- ☐ SHIT GOT REAL ★ ★ ★
- ☐ SAME SHIT DIFFERENT HOUSE ★ ★
- ☐ THINGS JUST DIDN'T COME OUT RIGHT ★

THOUGHTS/MESSAGES: _____
_____

Welcome! PLEASE SEAT YOURSELF AND ENJOY YOUR VISIT!

NAME: _____ DATE: _____ TIME: _____ DURATION OF VISIT: _____
HRS   MIN   SEC

PURPOSE FOR VISIT: ☐ #1 ☐ #2 ☐ OTHER: _____ SUCCESS? ☐ YES ☐ NO

FAVORITE EUPHEMISM FOR PERFORMING #1:

FAVORITE EUPHEMISM FOR PERFORMING #2:

FAVORITE RESTROOM GRAFFITI OR YOUR ORIGNAL DOODLE:

WHILE YOU WERE HERE, DID YOU:
- ☐ TEXT SOMEONE
- ☐ MAKE A PHONE CALL
- ☐ EMAIL
- ☐ CHECK SOCIAL MEDIA
- ☐ TAKE A SELFIE
- ☐ LOOK IN THE MEDICINE CABINET
- ☐ CHECK YOUR TEETH
- ☐ CHECK OUT YOUR BUTT
- ☐ CHECK YOUR FLY
- ☐ READ
- ☐ FIX YOUR HAIR
- ☐ TAKE SOME EXTRA "ME TIME"
- ☐ TALK TO YOURSELF
- ☐ CONDUCT BUSINESS OTHER THAN YOUR "BUSINESS." CARE TO SHARE?

FAVORITE NAME FOR THIS ROOM:
- ☐ BATHROOM
- ☐ TOILET
- ☐ POWDER ROOM
- ☐ LAVATORY
- ☐ SHITTER
- ☐ LOO
- ☐ LITTLE GIRLS ROOM
- ☐ LITTLE BOYS ROOM
- ☐ COMFORT STATION
- ☐ OTHER: _____
- ☐ JOHN
- ☐ CAN
- ☐ HEAD
- ☐ POTTY
- ☐ CRAPPER
- ☐ WC

RATINGS: 1 2 3 4 5
CLEANLINESS   ☆ ☆ ☆ ☆ ☆
AMBIENCE   ☆ ☆ ☆ ☆ ☆
AMENITIES   ☆ ☆ ☆ ☆ ☆
SOUND PROOFING   ☆ ☆ ☆ ☆ ☆
QUALITY OF THE FLUSH ☆ ☆ ☆ ☆ ☆
TOILET PAPER   ☆ ☆ ☆ ☆ ☆

OVERALL EXPERIENCE:
- ☐ BEST SEAT IN THE HOUSE   ★ ★ ★ ★ ★
- ☐ WOULD POOP HERE AGAIN   ★ ★ ★ ★
- ☐ SHIT GOT REAL   ★ ★ ★
- ☐ SAME SHIT DIFFERENT HOUSE   ★ ★
- ☐ THINGS JUST DIDN'T COME OUT RIGHT ★

THOUGHTS/MESSAGES: _____
_____
_____

Welcome! PLEASE SEAT YOURSELF AND ENJOY YOUR VISIT!

NAME: _____ DATE: _____ TIME: _____ DURATION OF VISIT: _____
HRS   MIN   SEC

PURPOSE FOR VISIT: ☐ #1 ☐ #2 ☐ OTHER: _____ SUCCESS? ☐ YES ☐ NO

FAVORITE EUPHEMISM FOR PERFORMING #1:

FAVORITE RESTROOM GRAFFITI OR YOUR ORIGNAL DOODLE:

FAVORITE EUPHEMISM FOR PERFORMING #2:

WHILE YOU WERE HERE, DID YOU:
- ☐ TEXT SOMEONE
- ☐ MAKE A PHONE CALL
- ☐ EMAIL
- ☐ CHECK SOCIAL MEDIA
- ☐ TAKE A SELFIE
- ☐ LOOK IN THE MEDICINE CABINET
- ☐ CHECK YOUR TEETH
- ☐ CHECK OUT YOUR BUTT
- ☐ CHECK YOUR FLY
- ☐ READ
- ☐ FIX YOUR HAIR
- ☐ TAKE SOME EXTRA "ME TIME"
- ☐ TALK TO YOURSELF
- ☐ CONDUCT BUSINESS OTHER THAN YOUR "BUSINESS." CARE TO SHARE?
  _____

FAVORITE NAME FOR THIS ROOM:
- ☐ BATHROOM
- ☐ TOILET
- ☐ POWDER ROOM
- ☐ LAVATORY
- ☐ SHITTER
- ☐ LOO
- ☐ LITTLE GIRLS ROOM
- ☐ LITTLE BOYS ROOM
- ☐ COMFORT STATION
- ☐ OTHER: _____
- ☐ JOHN
- ☐ CAN
- ☐ HEAD
- ☐ POTTY
- ☐ CRAPPER
- ☐ WC

_____

THOUGHTS/MESSAGES: _____
_____
_____

RATINGS: 1 2 3 4 5
CLEANLINESS   ☆ ☆ ☆ ☆ ☆
AMBIENCE   ☆ ☆ ☆ ☆ ☆
AMENITIES   ☆ ☆ ☆ ☆ ☆
SOUND PROOFING   ☆ ☆ ☆ ☆ ☆
QUALITY OF THE FLUSH ☆ ☆ ☆ ☆ ☆
TOILET PAPER   ☆ ☆ ☆ ☆ ☆

OVERALL EXPERIENCE:
- ☐ BEST SEAT IN THE HOUSE ★ ★ ★ ★ ★
- ☐ WOULD POOP HERE AGAIN ★ ★ ★ ★
- ☐ SHIT GOT REAL ★ ★ ★
- ☐ SAME SHIT DIFFERENT HOUSE ★ ★
- ☐ THINGS JUST DIDN'T COME OUT RIGHT ★

Welcome! PLEASE SEAT YOURSELF AND ENJOY YOUR VISIT!

NAME: _____ DATE: _____ TIME: _____ DURATION OF VISIT: _____

HRS   MIN   SEC

PURPOSE FOR VISIT: 🧻 #1 🧻 #2 🧻 OTHER: _____ SUCCESS? 🧻 YES 🧻 NO

FAVORITE EUPHEMISM FOR PERFORMING #1:

FAVORITE RESTROOM GRAFFITI OR YOUR ORIGNAL DOODLE:

FAVORITE EUPHEMISM FOR PERFORMING #2:

WHILE YOU WERE HERE, DID YOU:
- ☐ TEXT SOMEONE
- ☐ MAKE A PHONE CALL
- ☐ EMAIL
- ☐ CHECK SOCIAL MEDIA
- ☐ TAKE A SELFIE
- ☐ LOOK IN THE MEDICINE CABINET
- ☐ CHECK YOUR TEETH
- ☐ CHECK OUT YOUR BUTT
- ☐ CHECK YOUR FLY
- ☐ READ
- ☐ FIX YOUR HAIR
- ☐ TAKE SOME EXTRA "ME TIME"
- ☐ TALK TO YOURSELF
- ☐ CONDUCT BUSINESS OTHER THAN YOUR "BUSINESS." CARE TO SHARE?
_____

FAVORITE NAME FOR THIS ROOM:
- ☐ BATHROOM
- ☐ TOILET
- ☐ POWDER ROOM
- ☐ LAVATORY
- ☐ SHITTER
- ☐ LOO
- ☐ LITTLE GIRLS ROOM
- ☐ LITTLE BOYS ROOM
- ☐ COMFORT STATION
- ☐ OTHER: _____
_____

- ☐ JOHN
- ☐ CAN
- ☐ HEAD
- ☐ POTTY
- ☐ CRAPPER
- ☐ WC

RATINGS:
	1	2	3	4	5
CLEANLINESS	☆	☆	☆	☆	☆
AMBIENCE	☆	☆	☆	☆	☆
AMENITIES	☆	☆	☆	☆	☆
SOUND PROOFING	☆	☆	☆	☆	☆
QUALITY OF THE FLUSH	☆	☆	☆	☆	☆
TOILET PAPER	☆	☆	☆	☆	☆

OVERALL EXPERIENCE:
- ☐ BEST SEAT IN THE HOUSE ★ ★ ★ ★ ★
- ☐ WOULD POOP HERE AGAIN ★ ★ ★ ★
- ☐ SHIT GOT REAL ★ ★ ★
- ☐ SAME SHIT DIFFERENT HOUSE ★ ★
- ☐ THINGS JUST DIDN'T COME OUT RIGHT ★

THOUGHTS/MESSAGES: _____
_____
_____

Welcome! PLEASE SEAT YOURSELF AND ENJOY YOUR VISIT!

NAME: _____ DATE: _____ TIME: _____ DURATION OF VISIT: _____
HRS   MIN   SEC

PURPOSE FOR VISIT: 🧻 #1   🧻 #2   🧻 OTHER: _____   SUCCESS? 🧻 YES 🧻 NO

FAVORITE EUPHEMISM FOR PERFORMING #1:

FAVORITE RESTROOM GRAFFITI OR YOUR ORIGNAL DOODLE:

FAVORITE EUPHEMISM FOR PERFORMING #2:

WHILE YOU WERE HERE, DID YOU:
- ☐ TEXT SOMEONE
- ☐ MAKE A PHONE CALL
- ☐ EMAIL
- ☐ CHECK SOCIAL MEDIA
- ☐ TAKE A SELFIE
- ☐ LOOK IN THE MEDICINE CABINET
- ☐ CHECK YOUR TEETH
- ☐ CHECK OUT YOUR BUTT
- ☐ CHECK YOUR FLY
- ☐ READ
- ☐ FIX YOUR HAIR
- ☐ TAKE SOME EXTRA "ME TIME"
- ☐ TALK TO YOURSELF
- ☐ CONDUCT BUSINESS OTHER THAN YOUR "BUSINESS." CARE TO SHARE?
_____

FAVORITE NAME FOR THIS ROOM:
- ☐ BATHROOM
- ☐ TOILET
- ☐ POWDER ROOM
- ☐ LAVATORY
- ☐ SHITTER
- ☐ LOO
- ☐ LITTLE GIRLS ROOM
- ☐ LITTLE BOYS ROOM
- ☐ COMFORT STATION
- ☐ OTHER: _____
- ☐ JOHN
- ☐ CAN
- ☐ HEAD
- ☐ POTTY
- ☐ CRAPPER
- ☐ WC

_____

THOUGHTS/MESSAGES: _____
_____
_____

RATINGS: 1 2 3 4 5
CLEANLINESS   ☆ ☆ ☆ ☆ ☆
AMBIENCE   ☆ ☆ ☆ ☆ ☆
AMENITIES   ☆ ☆ ☆ ☆ ☆
SOUND PROOFING   ☆ ☆ ☆ ☆ ☆
QUALITY OF THE FLUSH ☆ ☆ ☆ ☆ ☆
TOILET PAPER   ☆ ☆ ☆ ☆ ☆

OVERALL EXPERIENCE:
- ☐ BEST SEAT IN THE HOUSE   ★ ★ ★ ★ ★
- ☐ WOULD POOP HERE AGAIN   ★ ★ ★ ★
- ☐ SHIT GOT REAL   ★ ★ ★
- ☐ SAME SHIT DIFFERENT HOUSE   ★ ★
- ☐ THINGS JUST DIDN'T COME OUT RIGHT ★

Welcome! PLEASE SEAT YOURSELF AND ENJOY YOUR VISIT!

NAME: _____ DATE: _____ TIME: _____ DURATION OF VISIT: _____
HRS   MIN   SEC

PURPOSE FOR VISIT: ☐ #1 ☐ #2 ☐ OTHER: _____ SUCCESS? ☐ YES ☐ NO

FAVORITE EUPHEMISM FOR PERFORMING #1: | FAVORITE RESTROOM GRAFFITI OR YOUR ORIGNAL DOODLE:

FAVORITE EUPHEMISM FOR PERFORMING #2:

WHILE YOU WERE HERE, DID YOU:
- ☐ TEXT SOMEONE
- ☐ MAKE A PHONE CALL
- ☐ EMAIL
- ☐ CHECK SOCIAL MEDIA
- ☐ TAKE A SELFIE
- ☐ LOOK IN THE MEDICINE CABINET
- ☐ CHECK YOUR TEETH
- ☐ CHECK OUT YOUR BUTT
- ☐ CHECK YOUR FLY
- ☐ READ
- ☐ FIX YOUR HAIR
- ☐ TAKE SOME EXTRA "ME TIME"
- ☐ TALK TO YOURSELF
- ☐ CONDUCT BUSINESS OTHER THAN YOUR "BUSINESS." CARE TO SHARE?
  _____

FAVORITE NAME FOR THIS ROOM:
- ☐ BATHROOM
- ☐ TOILET
- ☐ POWDER ROOM
- ☐ LAVATORY
- ☐ SHITTER
- ☐ LOO
- ☐ LITTLE GIRLS ROOM
- ☐ LITTLE BOYS ROOM
- ☐ COMFORT STATION
- ☐ OTHER: _____
  _____
- ☐ JOHN
- ☐ CAN
- ☐ HEAD
- ☐ POTTY
- ☐ CRAPPER
- ☐ WC

RATINGS: 1 2 3 4 5
CLEANLINESS   ☆ ☆ ☆ ☆ ☆
AMBIENCE   ☆ ☆ ☆ ☆ ☆
AMENITIES   ☆ ☆ ☆ ☆ ☆
SOUND PROOFING   ☆ ☆ ☆ ☆ ☆
QUALITY OF THE FLUSH ☆ ☆ ☆ ☆ ☆
TOILET PAPER   ☆ ☆ ☆ ☆ ☆

OVERALL EXPERIENCE:
- ☐ BEST SEAT IN THE HOUSE ★ ★ ★ ★ ★
- ☐ WOULD POOP HERE AGAIN ★ ★ ★ ★
- ☐ SHIT GOT REAL ★ ★ ★
- ☐ SAME SHIT DIFFERENT HOUSE ★ ★
- ☐ THINGS JUST DIDN'T COME OUT RIGHT ★

THOUGHTS/MESSAGES: _____
_____
_____

Welcome! PLEASE SEAT YOURSELF AND ENJOY YOUR VISIT!

NAME: _____ DATE: _____ TIME: _____ DURATION OF VISIT: _____
                                                                          HRS   MIN   SEC

PURPOSE FOR VISIT: ☐ #1 ☐ #2 ☐ OTHER: _____ SUCCESS? ☐ YES ☐ NO

FAVORITE EUPHEMISM FOR PERFORMING #1:

FAVORITE EUPHEMISM FOR PERFORMING #2:

FAVORITE RESTROOM GRAFFITI OR YOUR ORIGNAL DOODLE:

WHILE YOU WERE HERE, DID YOU:
☐ TEXT SOMEONE
☐ MAKE A PHONE CALL
☐ EMAIL
☐ CHECK SOCIAL MEDIA
☐ TAKE A SELFIE
☐ LOOK IN THE MEDICINE CABINET
☐ CHECK YOUR TEETH
☐ CHECK OUT YOUR BUTT
☐ CHECK YOUR FLY
☐ READ
☐ FIX YOUR HAIR
☐ TAKE SOME EXTRA "ME TIME"
☐ TALK TO YOURSELF
☐ CONDUCT BUSINESS OTHER THAN YOUR "BUSINESS." CARE TO SHARE?
_____

FAVORITE NAME FOR THIS ROOM:
☐ BATHROOM   ☐ JOHN
☐ TOILET   ☐ CAN
☐ POWDER ROOM   ☐ HEAD
☐ LAVATORY   ☐ POTTY
☐ SHITTER   ☐ CRAPPER
☐ LOO   ☐ WC
☐ LITTLE GIRLS ROOM
☐ LITTLE BOYS ROOM
☐ COMFORT STATION
☐ OTHER: _____
_____

RATINGS:
	1	2	3	4	5
CLEANLINESS	☆	☆	☆	☆	☆
AMBIENCE	☆	☆	☆	☆	☆
AMENITIES	☆	☆	☆	☆	☆
SOUND PROOFING	☆	☆	☆	☆	☆
QUALITY OF THE FLUSH	☆	☆	☆	☆	☆
TOILET PAPER	☆	☆	☆	☆	☆

OVERALL EXPERIENCE:
☐ BEST SEAT IN THE HOUSE ★★★★★
☐ WOULD POOP HERE AGAIN ★★★★
☐ SHIT GOT REAL ★★★
☐ SAME SHIT DIFFERENT HOUSE ★★
☐ THINGS JUST DIDN'T COME OUT RIGHT ★

THOUGHTS/MESSAGES: _____
_____
_____

Welcome! PLEASE SEAT YOURSELF AND ENJOY YOUR VISIT!

NAME: _____ DATE: _____ TIME: _____ DURATION OF VISIT: _____
HRS MIN SEC

PURPOSE FOR VISIT: 🧻 #1 🧻 #2 🧻 OTHER: _____ SUCCESS? 🧻 YES 🧻 NO

FAVORITE EUPHEMISM FOR PERFORMING #1:

FAVORITE RESTROOM GRAFFITI OR YOUR ORIGNAL DOODLE:

FAVORITE EUPHEMISM FOR PERFORMING #2:

WHILE YOU WERE HERE, DID YOU:
- ☐ TEXT SOMEONE
- ☐ MAKE A PHONE CALL
- ☐ EMAIL
- ☐ CHECK SOCIAL MEDIA
- ☐ TAKE A SELFIE
- ☐ LOOK IN THE MEDICINE CABINET
- ☐ CHECK YOUR TEETH
- ☐ CHECK OUT YOUR BUTT
- ☐ CHECK YOUR FLY
- ☐ READ
- ☐ FIX YOUR HAIR
- ☐ TAKE SOME EXTRA "ME TIME"
- ☐ TALK TO YOURSELF
- ☐ CONDUCT BUSINESS OTHER THAN YOUR "BUSINESS." CARE TO SHARE?

FAVORITE NAME FOR THIS ROOM:
- ☐ BATHROOM
- ☐ TOILET
- ☐ POWDER ROOM
- ☐ LAVATORY
- ☐ SHITTER
- ☐ LOO
- ☐ LITTLE GIRLS ROOM
- ☐ LITTLE BOYS ROOM
- ☐ COMFORT STATION
- ☐ OTHER: _____
- ☐ JOHN
- ☐ CAN
- ☐ HEAD
- ☐ POTTY
- ☐ CRAPPER
- ☐ WC

RATINGS:
	1	2	3	4	5
CLEANLINESS	☆	☆	☆	☆	☆
AMBIENCE	☆	☆	☆	☆	☆
AMENITIES	☆	☆	☆	☆	☆
SOUND PROOFING	☆	☆	☆	☆	☆
QUALITY OF THE FLUSH	☆	☆	☆	☆	☆
TOILET PAPER	☆	☆	☆	☆	☆

OVERALL EXPERIENCE:
- ☐ BEST SEAT IN THE HOUSE ★ ★ ★ ★ ★
- ☐ WOULD POOP HERE AGAIN ★ ★ ★ ★
- ☐ SHIT GOT REAL ★ ★ ★
- ☐ SAME SHIT DIFFERENT HOUSE ★ ★
- ☐ THINGS JUST DIDN'T COME OUT RIGHT ★

THOUGHTS/MESSAGES: _____
_____
_____

Welcome! PLEASE SEAT YOURSELF AND ENJOY YOUR VISIT!

NAME: _____ DATE: _____ TIME: _____ DURATION OF VISIT: _____
HRS   MIN   SEC

PURPOSE FOR VISIT: 🧻 #1 🧻 #2 🧻 OTHER: _____ SUCCESS? 🧻 YES 🧻 NO

FAVORITE EUPHEMISM FOR PERFORMING #1:

FAVORITE RESTROOM GRAFFITI OR YOUR ORIGNAL DOODLE:

FAVORITE EUPHEMISM FOR PERFORMING #2:

WHILE YOU WERE HERE, DID YOU:
☐ TEXT SOMEONE
☐ MAKE A PHONE CALL
☐ EMAIL
☐ CHECK SOCIAL MEDIA
☐ TAKE A SELFIE
☐ LOOK IN THE MEDICINE CABINET
☐ CHECK YOUR TEETH
☐ CHECK OUT YOUR BUTT
☐ CHECK YOUR FLY
☐ READ
☐ FIX YOUR HAIR
☐ TAKE SOME EXTRA "ME TIME"
☐ TALK TO YOURSELF
☐ CONDUCT BUSINESS OTHER THAN YOUR "BUSINESS." CARE TO SHARE?
_____

FAVORITE NAME FOR THIS ROOM:
☐ BATHROOM   ☐ JOHN
☐ TOILET   ☐ CAN
☐ POWDER ROOM   ☐ HEAD
☐ LAVATORY   ☐ POTTY
☐ SHITTER   ☐ CRAPPER
☐ LOO   ☐ WC
☐ LITTLE GIRLS ROOM
☐ LITTLE BOYS ROOM
☐ COMFORT STATION
☐ OTHER: _____
_____

RATINGS:
	1	2	3	4	5
CLEANLINESS	☆	☆	☆	☆	☆
AMBIENCE	☆	☆	☆	☆	☆
AMENITIES	☆	☆	☆	☆	☆
SOUND PROOFING	☆	☆	☆	☆	☆
QUALITY OF THE FLUSH	☆	☆	☆	☆	☆
TOILET PAPER	☆	☆	☆	☆	☆

OVERALL EXPERIENCE:
☐ BEST SEAT IN THE HOUSE ★ ★ ★ ★ ★
☐ WOULD POOP HERE AGAIN ★ ★ ★ ★
☐ SHIT GOT REAL ★ ★ ★
☐ SAME SHIT DIFFERENT HOUSE ★ ★
☐ THINGS JUST DIDN'T COME OUT RIGHT ★

THOUGHTS/MESSAGES: _____
_____
_____

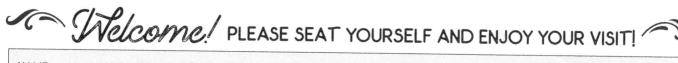

Welcome! PLEASE SEAT YOURSELF AND ENJOY YOUR VISIT!

NAME: _____ DATE: _____ TIME: _____ DURATION OF VISIT: _____
HRS   MIN   SEC

PURPOSE FOR VISIT: 🧻 #1 🧻 #2 🧻 OTHER: _____ SUCCESS? 🧻 YES 🧻 NO

FAVORITE EUPHEMISM FOR PERFORMING #1:

FAVORITE RESTROOM GRAFFITI OR YOUR ORIGNAL DOODLE:

FAVORITE EUPHEMISM FOR PERFORMING #2:

WHILE YOU WERE HERE, DID YOU:
- ☐ TEXT SOMEONE
- ☐ MAKE A PHONE CALL
- ☐ EMAIL
- ☐ CHECK SOCIAL MEDIA
- ☐ TAKE A SELFIE
- ☐ LOOK IN THE MEDICINE CABINET
- ☐ CHECK YOUR TEETH
- ☐ CHECK OUT YOUR BUTT
- ☐ CHECK YOUR FLY
- ☐ READ
- ☐ FIX YOUR HAIR
- ☐ TAKE SOME EXTRA "ME TIME"
- ☐ TALK TO YOURSELF
- ☐ CONDUCT BUSINESS OTHER THAN YOUR "BUSINESS." CARE TO SHARE?

FAVORITE NAME FOR THIS ROOM:
- ☐ BATHROOM
- ☐ TOILET
- ☐ POWDER ROOM
- ☐ LAVATORY
- ☐ SHITTER
- ☐ LOO
- ☐ LITTLE GIRLS ROOM
- ☐ LITTLE BOYS ROOM
- ☐ COMFORT STATION
- ☐ OTHER: _____
- ☐ JOHN
- ☐ CAN
- ☐ HEAD
- ☐ POTTY
- ☐ CRAPPER
- ☐ WC

RATINGS:
	1	2	3	4	5
CLEANLINESS	☆	☆	☆	☆	☆
AMBIENCE	☆	☆	☆	☆	☆
AMENITIES	☆	☆	☆	☆	☆
SOUND PROOFING	☆	☆	☆	☆	☆
QUALITY OF THE FLUSH	☆	☆	☆	☆	☆
TOILET PAPER	☆	☆	☆	☆	☆

OVERALL EXPERIENCE:
- ☐ BEST SEAT IN THE HOUSE ★ ★ ★ ★ ★
- ☐ WOULD POOP HERE AGAIN ★ ★ ★ ★
- ☐ SHIT GOT REAL ★ ★ ★
- ☐ SAME SHIT DIFFERENT HOUSE ★ ★
- ☐ THINGS JUST DIDN'T COME OUT RIGHT ★

THOUGHTS/MESSAGES: _____
_____

Welcome! PLEASE SEAT YOURSELF AND ENJOY YOUR VISIT!

NAME: _____ DATE: _____ TIME: _____ DURATION OF VISIT: _____
HRS   MIN   SEC

PURPOSE FOR VISIT: 🧻 #1   🧻 #2   🧻 OTHER: _____   SUCCESS? 🧻 YES 🧻 NO

FAVORITE EUPHEMISM FOR PERFORMING #1:

FAVORITE RESTROOM GRAFFITI OR YOUR ORIGNAL DOODLE:

FAVORITE EUPHEMISM FOR PERFORMING #2:

WHILE YOU WERE HERE, DID YOU:
- ☐ TEXT SOMEONE
- ☐ MAKE A PHONE CALL
- ☐ EMAIL
- ☐ CHECK SOCIAL MEDIA
- ☐ TAKE A SELFIE
- ☐ LOOK IN THE MEDICINE CABINET
- ☐ CHECK YOUR TEETH
- ☐ CHECK OUT YOUR BUTT
- ☐ CHECK YOUR FLY
- ☐ READ
- ☐ FIX YOUR HAIR
- ☐ TAKE SOME EXTRA "ME TIME"
- ☐ TALK TO YOURSELF
- ☐ CONDUCT BUSINESS OTHER THAN YOUR "BUSINESS." CARE TO SHARE?
  _____

FAVORITE NAME FOR THIS ROOM:
- ☐ BATHROOM
- ☐ TOILET
- ☐ POWDER ROOM
- ☐ LAVATORY
- ☐ SHITTER
- ☐ LOO
- ☐ LITTLE GIRLS ROOM
- ☐ LITTLE BOYS ROOM
- ☐ COMFORT STATION
- ☐ OTHER: _____
- ☐ JOHN
- ☐ CAN
- ☐ HEAD
- ☐ POTTY
- ☐ CRAPPER
- ☐ WC

_____

RATINGS:	1	2	3	4	5
CLEANLINESS	☆	☆	☆	☆	☆
AMBIENCE	☆	☆	☆	☆	☆
AMENITIES	☆	☆	☆	☆	☆
SOUND PROOFING	☆	☆	☆	☆	☆
QUALITY OF THE FLUSH	☆	☆	☆	☆	☆
TOILET PAPER	☆	☆	☆	☆	☆

OVERALL EXPERIENCE:
- ☐ BEST SEAT IN THE HOUSE ★★★★★
- ☐ WOULD POOP HERE AGAIN ★★★★
- ☐ SHIT GOT REAL ★★★
- ☐ SAME SHIT DIFFERENT HOUSE ★★
- ☐ THINGS JUST DIDN'T COME OUT RIGHT ★

THOUGHTS/MESSAGES: _____
_____
_____

Welcome! PLEASE SEAT YOURSELF AND ENJOY YOUR VISIT!

NAME: _____ DATE: _____ TIME: _____ DURATION OF VISIT: _____

HRS   MIN   SEC

PURPOSE FOR VISIT: ☐ #1   ☐ #2   ☐ OTHER: _____   SUCCESS? ☐ YES ☐ NO

FAVORITE EUPHEMISM FOR PERFORMING #1:

FAVORITE RESTROOM GRAFFITI OR YOUR ORIGNAL DOODLE:

FAVORITE EUPHEMISM FOR PERFORMING #2:

WHILE YOU WERE HERE, DID YOU:
☐ TEXT SOMEONE
☐ MAKE A PHONE CALL
☐ EMAIL
☐ CHECK SOCIAL MEDIA
☐ TAKE A SELFIE
☐ LOOK IN THE MEDICINE CABINET
☐ CHECK YOUR TEETH
☐ CHECK OUT YOUR BUTT
☐ CHECK YOUR FLY
☐ READ
☐ FIX YOUR HAIR
☐ TAKE SOME EXTRA "ME TIME"
☐ TALK TO YOURSELF
☐ CONDUCT BUSINESS OTHER THAN YOUR "BUSINESS." CARE TO SHARE?
_____

FAVORITE NAME FOR THIS ROOM:
☐ BATHROOM   ☐ JOHN
☐ TOILET   ☐ CAN
☐ POWDER ROOM   ☐ HEAD
☐ LAVATORY   ☐ POTTY
☐ SHITTER   ☐ CRAPPER
☐ LOO   ☐ WC
☐ LITTLE GIRLS ROOM
☐ LITTLE BOYS ROOM
☐ COMFORT STATION
☐ OTHER: _____

THOUGHTS/MESSAGES: _____
_____
_____

RATINGS:
	1	2	3	4	5
CLEANLINESS	☆	☆	☆	☆	☆
AMBIENCE	☆	☆	☆	☆	☆
AMENITIES	☆	☆	☆	☆	☆
SOUND PROOFING	☆	☆	☆	☆	☆
QUALITY OF THE FLUSH	☆	☆	☆	☆	☆
TOILET PAPER	☆	☆	☆	☆	☆

OVERALL EXPERIENCE:
☐ BEST SEAT IN THE HOUSE ★★★★★
☐ WOULD POOP HERE AGAIN ★★★★
☐ SHIT GOT REAL ★★★
☐ SAME SHIT DIFFERENT HOUSE ★★
☐ THINGS JUST DIDN'T COME OUT RIGHT ★

Welcome! PLEASE SEAT YOURSELF AND ENJOY YOUR VISIT!

NAME: _____ DATE: _____ TIME: _____ DURATION OF VISIT: _____
HRS   MIN   SEC

PURPOSE FOR VISIT: 🧻 #1 🧻 #2 🧻 OTHER: _____ SUCCESS? 🧻 YES 🧻 NO

FAVORITE EUPHEMISM FOR PERFORMING #1:

FAVORITE RESTROOM GRAFFITI OR YOUR ORIGNAL DOODLE:

FAVORITE EUPHEMISM FOR PERFORMING #2:

WHILE YOU WERE HERE, DID YOU:
- ☐ TEXT SOMEONE
- ☐ MAKE A PHONE CALL
- ☐ EMAIL
- ☐ CHECK SOCIAL MEDIA
- ☐ TAKE A SELFIE
- ☐ LOOK IN THE MEDICINE CABINET
- ☐ CHECK YOUR TEETH
- ☐ CHECK OUT YOUR BUTT
- ☐ CHECK YOUR FLY
- ☐ READ
- ☐ FIX YOUR HAIR
- ☐ TAKE SOME EXTRA "ME TIME"
- ☐ TALK TO YOURSELF
- ☐ CONDUCT BUSINESS OTHER THAN YOUR "BUSINESS." CARE TO SHARE?
  _____

FAVORITE NAME FOR THIS ROOM:
- ☐ BATHROOM
- ☐ TOILET
- ☐ POWDER ROOM
- ☐ LAVATORY
- ☐ SHITTER
- ☐ LOO
- ☐ LITTLE GIRLS ROOM
- ☐ LITTLE BOYS ROOM
- ☐ COMFORT STATION
- ☐ OTHER: _____
- ☐ JOHN
- ☐ CAN
- ☐ HEAD
- ☐ POTTY
- ☐ CRAPPER
- ☐ WC

RATINGS: 1 2 3 4 5
- CLEANLINESS   ☆ ☆ ☆ ☆ ☆
- AMBIENCE   ☆ ☆ ☆ ☆ ☆
- AMENITIES   ☆ ☆ ☆ ☆ ☆
- SOUND PROOFING   ☆ ☆ ☆ ☆ ☆
- QUALITY OF THE FLUSH ☆ ☆ ☆ ☆ ☆
- TOILET PAPER   ☆ ☆ ☆ ☆ ☆

OVERALL EXPERIENCE:
- ☐ BEST SEAT IN THE HOUSE ★ ★ ★ ★ ★
- ☐ WOULD POOP HERE AGAIN ★ ★ ★ ★
- ☐ SHIT GOT REAL ★ ★ ★
- ☐ SAME SHIT DIFFERENT HOUSE ★ ★
- ☐ THINGS JUST DIDN'T COME OUT RIGHT ★

THOUGHTS/MESSAGES: _____
_____

Welcome! PLEASE SEAT YOURSELF AND ENJOY YOUR VISIT!

NAME: _____ DATE: _____ TIME: _____ DURATION OF VISIT: _____
HRS   MIN   SEC

PURPOSE FOR VISIT: 🧻 #1   🧻 #2   🧻 OTHER: _____   SUCCESS? 🧻 YES 🧻 NO

FAVORITE EUPHEMISM FOR PERFORMING #1:

FAVORITE RESTROOM GRAFFITI OR YOUR ORIGNAL DOODLE:

FAVORITE EUPHEMISM FOR PERFORMING #2:

WHILE YOU WERE HERE, DID YOU:
- ☐ TEXT SOMEONE
- ☐ MAKE A PHONE CALL
- ☐ EMAIL
- ☐ CHECK SOCIAL MEDIA
- ☐ TAKE A SELFIE
- ☐ LOOK IN THE MEDICINE CABINET
- ☐ CHECK YOUR TEETH
- ☐ CHECK OUT YOUR BUTT
- ☐ CHECK YOUR FLY
- ☐ READ
- ☐ FIX YOUR HAIR
- ☐ TAKE SOME EXTRA "ME TIME"
- ☐ TALK TO YOURSELF
- ☐ CONDUCT BUSINESS OTHER THAN YOUR "BUSINESS." CARE TO SHARE?

FAVORITE NAME FOR THIS ROOM:
- ☐ BATHROOM
- ☐ TOILET
- ☐ POWDER ROOM
- ☐ LAVATORY
- ☐ SHITTER
- ☐ LOO
- ☐ LITTLE GIRLS ROOM
- ☐ LITTLE BOYS ROOM
- ☐ COMFORT STATION
- ☐ OTHER: _____
- ☐ JOHN
- ☐ CAN
- ☐ HEAD
- ☐ POTTY
- ☐ CRAPPER
- ☐ WC

THOUGHTS/MESSAGES: _____

RATINGS: 1 2 3 4 5
CLEANLINESS   ☆ ☆ ☆ ☆ ☆
AMBIENCE   ☆ ☆ ☆ ☆ ☆
AMENITIES   ☆ ☆ ☆ ☆ ☆
SOUND PROOFING   ☆ ☆ ☆ ☆ ☆
QUALITY OF THE FLUSH ☆ ☆ ☆ ☆ ☆
TOILET PAPER   ☆ ☆ ☆ ☆ ☆

OVERALL EXPERIENCE:
- ☐ BEST SEAT IN THE HOUSE   ★ ★ ★ ★ ★
- ☐ WOULD POOP HERE AGAIN   ★ ★ ★ ★
- ☐ SHIT GOT REAL   ★ ★ ★
- ☐ SAME SHIT DIFFERENT HOUSE   ★ ★
- ☐ THINGS JUST DIDN'T COME OUT RIGHT ★

Welcome! PLEASE SEAT YOURSELF AND ENJOY YOUR VISIT!

NAME: _____ DATE: _____ TIME: _____ DURATION OF VISIT: _____
HRS   MIN   SEC

PURPOSE FOR VISIT: 🧻 #1   🧻 #2   🧻 OTHER: _____   SUCCESS? 🧻 YES 🧻 NO

FAVORITE EUPHEMISM FOR PERFORMING #1:

FAVORITE RESTROOM GRAFFITI OR YOUR ORIGNAL DOODLE:

FAVORITE EUPHEMISM FOR PERFORMING #2:

WHILE YOU WERE HERE, DID YOU:
- ☐ TEXT SOMEONE
- ☐ MAKE A PHONE CALL
- ☐ EMAIL
- ☐ CHECK SOCIAL MEDIA
- ☐ TAKE A SELFIE
- ☐ LOOK IN THE MEDICINE CABINET
- ☐ CHECK YOUR TEETH
- ☐ CHECK OUT YOUR BUTT
- ☐ CHECK YOUR FLY
- ☐ READ
- ☐ FIX YOUR HAIR
- ☐ TAKE SOME EXTRA "ME TIME"
- ☐ TALK TO YOURSELF
- ☐ CONDUCT BUSINESS OTHER THAN YOUR "BUSINESS." CARE TO SHARE?
_____

FAVORITE NAME FOR THIS ROOM:
- ☐ BATHROOM
- ☐ TOILET
- ☐ POWDER ROOM
- ☐ LAVATORY
- ☐ SHITTER
- ☐ LOO
- ☐ LITTLE GIRLS ROOM
- ☐ LITTLE BOYS ROOM
- ☐ COMFORT STATION
- ☐ OTHER: _____

- ☐ JOHN
- ☐ CAN
- ☐ HEAD
- ☐ POTTY
- ☐ CRAPPER
- ☐ WC

RATINGS:
	1 2 3 4 5
CLEANLINESS	☆ ☆ ☆ ☆ ☆
AMBIENCE	☆ ☆ ☆ ☆ ☆
AMENITIES	☆ ☆ ☆ ☆ ☆
SOUND PROOFING	☆ ☆ ☆ ☆ ☆
QUALITY OF THE FLUSH	☆ ☆ ☆ ☆ ☆
TOILET PAPER	☆ ☆ ☆ ☆ ☆

OVERALL EXPERIENCE:
- ☐ BEST SEAT IN THE HOUSE ★ ★ ★ ★ ★
- ☐ WOULD POOP HERE AGAIN ★ ★ ★ ★
- ☐ SHIT GOT REAL ★ ★ ★
- ☐ SAME SHIT DIFFERENT HOUSE ★ ★
- ☐ THINGS JUST DIDN'T COME OUT RIGHT ★

THOUGHTS/MESSAGES: _____
_____
_____

Welcome! PLEASE SEAT YOURSELF AND ENJOY YOUR VISIT!

NAME: _____ DATE: _____ TIME: _____ DURATION OF VISIT: _____
                                                                                    HRS   MIN   SEC

PURPOSE FOR VISIT: 🧻 #1 🧻 #2 🧻 OTHER: _____ SUCCESS? 🧻 YES 🧻 NO

FAVORITE EUPHEMISM FOR PERFORMING #1: | FAVORITE RESTROOM GRAFFITI OR YOUR ORIGNAL DOODLE:

FAVORITE EUPHEMISM FOR PERFORMING #2:

WHILE YOU WERE HERE, DID YOU:
- ☐ TEXT SOMEONE
- ☐ MAKE A PHONE CALL
- ☐ EMAIL
- ☐ CHECK SOCIAL MEDIA
- ☐ TAKE A SELFIE
- ☐ LOOK IN THE MEDICINE CABINET
- ☐ CHECK YOUR TEETH
- ☐ CHECK OUT YOUR BUTT
- ☐ CHECK YOUR FLY
- ☐ READ
- ☐ FIX YOUR HAIR
- ☐ TAKE SOME EXTRA "ME TIME"
- ☐ TALK TO YOURSELF
- ☐ CONDUCT BUSINESS OTHER THAN YOUR "BUSINESS." CARE TO SHARE?
  _____

FAVORITE NAME FOR THIS ROOM:
- ☐ BATHROOM
- ☐ TOILET
- ☐ POWDER ROOM
- ☐ LAVATORY
- ☐ SHITTER
- ☐ LOO
- ☐ LITTLE GIRLS ROOM
- ☐ LITTLE BOYS ROOM
- ☐ COMFORT STATION
- ☐ OTHER: _____

- ☐ JOHN
- ☐ CAN
- ☐ HEAD
- ☐ POTTY
- ☐ CRAPPER
- ☐ WC

_____

THOUGHTS/MESSAGES: _____
_____
_____

RATINGS: 1 2 3 4 5
CLEANLINESS   ☆ ☆ ☆ ☆ ☆
AMBIENCE   ☆ ☆ ☆ ☆ ☆
AMENITIES   ☆ ☆ ☆ ☆ ☆
SOUND PROOFING   ☆ ☆ ☆ ☆ ☆
QUALITY OF THE FLUSH   ☆ ☆ ☆ ☆ ☆
TOILET PAPER   ☆ ☆ ☆ ☆ ☆

OVERALL EXPERIENCE:
- ☐ BEST SEAT IN THE HOUSE   ★ ★ ★ ★ ★
- ☐ WOULD POOP HERE AGAIN   ★ ★ ★ ★
- ☐ SHIT GOT REAL   ★ ★ ★
- ☐ SAME SHIT DIFFERENT HOUSE   ★ ★
- ☐ THINGS JUST DIDN'T COME OUT RIGHT   ★

Welcome! PLEASE SEAT YOURSELF AND ENJOY YOUR VISIT!

NAME: _____ DATE: _____ TIME: _____ DURATION OF VISIT: _____
                                                                                    HRS   MIN   SEC

PURPOSE FOR VISIT: ▢ #1 ▢ #2 ▢ OTHER: _____ SUCCESS? ▢ YES ▢ NO

FAVORITE EUPHEMISM FOR PERFORMING #1:

FAVORITE RESTROOM GRAFFITI OR YOUR ORIGNAL DOODLE:

FAVORITE EUPHEMISM FOR PERFORMING #2:

WHILE YOU WERE HERE, DID YOU:
- ▢ TEXT SOMEONE
- ▢ MAKE A PHONE CALL
- ▢ EMAIL
- ▢ CHECK SOCIAL MEDIA
- ▢ TAKE A SELFIE
- ▢ LOOK IN THE MEDICINE CABINET
- ▢ CHECK YOUR TEETH
- ▢ CHECK OUT YOUR BUTT
- ▢ CHECK YOUR FLY
- ▢ READ
- ▢ FIX YOUR HAIR
- ▢ TAKE SOME EXTRA "ME TIME"
- ▢ TALK TO YOURSELF
- ▢ CONDUCT BUSINESS OTHER THAN YOUR "BUSINESS." CARE TO SHARE?
  _____

FAVORITE NAME FOR THIS ROOM:
- ▢ BATHROOM
- ▢ TOILET
- ▢ POWDER ROOM
- ▢ LAVATORY
- ▢ SHITTER
- ▢ LOO
- ▢ LITTLE GIRLS ROOM
- ▢ LITTLE BOYS ROOM
- ▢ COMFORT STATION
- ▢ OTHER: _____
- ▢ JOHN
- ▢ CAN
- ▢ HEAD
- ▢ POTTY
- ▢ CRAPPER
- ▢ WC

RATINGS:	1	2	3	4	5
CLEANLINESS	☆	☆	☆	☆	☆
AMBIENCE	☆	☆	☆	☆	☆
AMENITIES	☆	☆	☆	☆	☆
SOUND PROOFING	☆	☆	☆	☆	☆
QUALITY OF THE FLUSH	☆	☆	☆	☆	☆
TOILET PAPER	☆	☆	☆	☆	☆

OVERALL EXPERIENCE:
- ▢ BEST SEAT IN THE HOUSE ★ ★ ★ ★ ★
- ▢ WOULD POOP HERE AGAIN ★ ★ ★ ★
- ▢ SHIT GOT REAL ★ ★ ★
- ▢ SAME SHIT DIFFERENT HOUSE ★ ★
- ▢ THINGS JUST DIDN'T COME OUT RIGHT ★

THOUGHTS/MESSAGES: _____
_____
_____

Welcome! PLEASE SEAT YOURSELF AND ENJOY YOUR VISIT!

NAME: _____ DATE: _____ TIME: _____ DURATION OF VISIT: _____
                                                           HRS   MIN   SEC

PURPOSE FOR VISIT: ☐ #1 ☐ #2 ☐ OTHER: _____ SUCCESS? ☐ YES ☐ NO

FAVORITE EUPHEMISM FOR PERFORMING #1:

FAVORITE RESTROOM GRAFFITI OR YOUR ORIGNAL DOODLE:

FAVORITE EUPHEMISM FOR PERFORMING #2:

WHILE YOU WERE HERE, DID YOU:
- ☐ TEXT SOMEONE
- ☐ MAKE A PHONE CALL
- ☐ EMAIL
- ☐ CHECK SOCIAL MEDIA
- ☐ TAKE A SELFIE
- ☐ LOOK IN THE MEDICINE CABINET
- ☐ CHECK YOUR TEETH
- ☐ CHECK OUT YOUR BUTT
- ☐ CHECK YOUR FLY
- ☐ READ
- ☐ FIX YOUR HAIR
- ☐ TAKE SOME EXTRA "ME TIME"
- ☐ TALK TO YOURSELF
- ☐ CONDUCT BUSINESS OTHER THAN YOUR "BUSINESS." CARE TO SHARE?
_____

FAVORITE NAME FOR THIS ROOM:
- ☐ BATHROOM
- ☐ TOILET
- ☐ POWDER ROOM
- ☐ LAVATORY
- ☐ SHITTER
- ☐ LOO
- ☐ LITTLE GIRLS ROOM
- ☐ LITTLE BOYS ROOM
- ☐ COMFORT STATION
- ☐ OTHER: _____

- ☐ JOHN
- ☐ CAN
- ☐ HEAD
- ☐ POTTY
- ☐ CRAPPER
- ☐ WC

_____

THOUGHTS/MESSAGES: _____
_____
_____

RATINGS:

	1	2	3	4	5
CLEANLINESS	☆	☆	☆	☆	☆
AMBIENCE	☆	☆	☆	☆	☆
AMENITIES	☆	☆	☆	☆	☆
SOUND PROOFING	☆	☆	☆	☆	☆
QUALITY OF THE FLUSH	☆	☆	☆	☆	☆
TOILET PAPER	☆	☆	☆	☆	☆

OVERALL EXPERIENCE:
- ☐ BEST SEAT IN THE HOUSE ★ ★ ★ ★ ★
- ☐ WOULD POOP HERE AGAIN ★ ★ ★ ★
- ☐ SHIT GOT REAL ★ ★ ★
- ☐ SAME SHIT DIFFERENT HOUSE ★ ★
- ☐ THINGS JUST DIDN'T COME OUT RIGHT ★

Welcome! PLEASE SEAT YOURSELF AND ENJOY YOUR VISIT!

NAME: _____ DATE: _____ TIME: _____ DURATION OF VISIT: _____
HRS   MIN   SEC

PURPOSE FOR VISIT: ☐ #1 ☐ #2 ☐ OTHER: _____ SUCCESS? ☐ YES ☐ NO

FAVORITE EUPHEMISM FOR PERFORMING #1:

FAVORITE RESTROOM GRAFFITI OR YOUR ORIGNAL DOODLE:

FAVORITE EUPHEMISM FOR PERFORMING #2:

WHILE YOU WERE HERE, DID YOU:
☐ TEXT SOMEONE
☐ MAKE A PHONE CALL
☐ EMAIL
☐ CHECK SOCIAL MEDIA
☐ TAKE A SELFIE
☐ LOOK IN THE MEDICINE CABINET
☐ CHECK YOUR TEETH
☐ CHECK OUT YOUR BUTT
☐ CHECK YOUR FLY
☐ READ
☐ FIX YOUR HAIR
☐ TAKE SOME EXTRA "ME TIME"
☐ TALK TO YOURSELF
☐ CONDUCT BUSINESS OTHER THAN YOUR "BUSINESS." CARE TO SHARE?
_____

FAVORITE NAME FOR THIS ROOM:
☐ BATHROOM   ☐ JOHN
☐ TOILET   ☐ CAN
☐ POWDER ROOM   ☐ HEAD
☐ LAVATORY   ☐ POTTY
☐ SHITTER   ☐ CRAPPER
☐ LOO   ☐ WC
☐ LITTLE GIRLS ROOM
☐ LITTLE BOYS ROOM
☐ COMFORT STATION
☐ OTHER: _____

RATINGS: 1 2 3 4 5
CLEANLINESS   ☆ ☆ ☆ ☆ ☆
AMBIENCE   ☆ ☆ ☆ ☆ ☆
AMENITIES   ☆ ☆ ☆ ☆ ☆
SOUND PROOFING   ☆ ☆ ☆ ☆ ☆
QUALITY OF THE FLUSH   ☆ ☆ ☆ ☆ ☆
TOILET PAPER   ☆ ☆ ☆ ☆ ☆

OVERALL EXPERIENCE:
☐ BEST SEAT IN THE HOUSE   ★ ★ ★ ★ ★
☐ WOULD POOP HERE AGAIN   ★ ★ ★ ★
☐ SHIT GOT REAL   ★ ★ ★
☐ SAME SHIT DIFFERENT HOUSE   ★ ★
☐ THINGS JUST DIDN'T COME OUT RIGHT ★

THOUGHTS/MESSAGES: _____
_____
_____

Welcome! PLEASE SEAT YOURSELF AND ENJOY YOUR VISIT!

NAME: _____ DATE: _____ TIME: _____ DURATION OF VISIT: _____

HRS   MIN   SEC

PURPOSE FOR VISIT: ☐ #1 ☐ #2 ☐ OTHER: _____ SUCCESS? ☐ YES ☐ NO

FAVORITE EUPHEMISM FOR PERFORMING #1:

FAVORITE RESTROOM GRAFFITI OR YOUR ORIGNAL DOODLE:

FAVORITE EUPHEMISM FOR PERFORMING #2:

WHILE YOU WERE HERE, DID YOU:
- ☐ TEXT SOMEONE
- ☐ MAKE A PHONE CALL
- ☐ EMAIL
- ☐ CHECK SOCIAL MEDIA
- ☐ TAKE A SELFIE
- ☐ LOOK IN THE MEDICINE CABINET
- ☐ CHECK YOUR TEETH
- ☐ CHECK OUT YOUR BUTT
- ☐ CHECK YOUR FLY
- ☐ READ
- ☐ FIX YOUR HAIR
- ☐ TAKE SOME EXTRA "ME TIME"
- ☐ TALK TO YOURSELF
- ☐ CONDUCT BUSINESS OTHER THAN YOUR "BUSINESS." CARE TO SHARE?

_____

FAVORITE NAME FOR THIS ROOM:
- ☐ BATHROOM
- ☐ TOILET
- ☐ POWDER ROOM
- ☐ LAVATORY
- ☐ SHITTER
- ☐ LOO
- ☐ LITTLE GIRLS ROOM
- ☐ LITTLE BOYS ROOM
- ☐ COMFORT STATION
- ☐ OTHER: _____
- ☐ JOHN
- ☐ CAN
- ☐ HEAD
- ☐ POTTY
- ☐ CRAPPER
- ☐ WC

_____

THOUGHTS/MESSAGES: _____

_____

_____

RATINGS:

	1	2	3	4	5
CLEANLINESS	☆	☆	☆	☆	☆
AMBIENCE	☆	☆	☆	☆	☆
AMENITIES	☆	☆	☆	☆	☆
SOUND PROOFING	☆	☆	☆	☆	☆
QUALITY OF THE FLUSH	☆	☆	☆	☆	☆
TOILET PAPER	☆	☆	☆	☆	☆

OVERALL EXPERIENCE:
- ☐ BEST SEAT IN THE HOUSE ★ ★ ★ ★ ★
- ☐ WOULD POOP HERE AGAIN ★ ★ ★ ★
- ☐ SHIT GOT REAL ★ ★ ★
- ☐ SAME SHIT DIFFERENT HOUSE ★ ★
- ☐ THINGS JUST DIDN'T COME OUT RIGHT ★

Welcome! PLEASE SEAT YOURSELF AND ENJOY YOUR VISIT!

NAME: _____ DATE: _____ TIME: _____ DURATION OF VISIT: _____
HRS   MIN   SEC

PURPOSE FOR VISIT: ☐ #1 ☐ #2 ☐ OTHER: _____ SUCCESS? ☐ YES ☐ NO

FAVORITE EUPHEMISM FOR PERFORMING #1:

FAVORITE RESTROOM GRAFFITI OR YOUR ORIGNAL DOODLE:

FAVORITE EUPHEMISM FOR PERFORMING #2:

WHILE YOU WERE HERE, DID YOU:
☐ TEXT SOMEONE
☐ MAKE A PHONE CALL
☐ EMAIL
☐ CHECK SOCIAL MEDIA
☐ TAKE A SELFIE
☐ LOOK IN THE MEDICINE CABINET
☐ CHECK YOUR TEETH
☐ CHECK OUT YOUR BUTT
☐ CHECK YOUR FLY
☐ READ
☐ FIX YOUR HAIR
☐ TAKE SOME EXTRA "ME TIME"
☐ TALK TO YOURSELF
☐ CONDUCT BUSINESS OTHER THAN YOUR "BUSINESS." CARE TO SHARE?
_____

FAVORITE NAME FOR THIS ROOM:
☐ BATHROOM   ☐ JOHN
☐ TOILET   ☐ CAN
☐ POWDER ROOM   ☐ HEAD
☐ LAVATORY   ☐ POTTY
☐ SHITTER   ☐ CRAPPER
☐ LOO   ☐ WC
☐ LITTLE GIRLS ROOM
☐ LITTLE BOYS ROOM
☐ COMFORT STATION
☐ OTHER: _____
_____

THOUGHTS/MESSAGES: _____
_____

RATINGS:
	1	2	3	4	5
CLEANLINESS	☆	☆	☆	☆	☆
AMBIENCE	☆	☆	☆	☆	☆
AMENITIES	☆	☆	☆	☆	☆
SOUND PROOFING	☆	☆	☆	☆	☆
QUALITY OF THE FLUSH	☆	☆	☆	☆	☆
TOILET PAPER	☆	☆	☆	☆	☆

OVERALL EXPERIENCE:
☐ BEST SEAT IN THE HOUSE ★ ★ ★ ★ ★
☐ WOULD POOP HERE AGAIN ★ ★ ★ ★
☐ SHIT GOT REAL ★ ★ ★
☐ SAME SHIT DIFFERENT HOUSE ★ ★
☐ THINGS JUST DIDN'T COME OUT RIGHT ★

Welcome! PLEASE SEAT YOURSELF AND ENJOY YOUR VISIT!

NAME: _____ DATE: _____ TIME: _____ DURATION OF VISIT: _____
HRS   MIN   SEC

PURPOSE FOR VISIT: ☐ #1 ☐ #2 ☐ OTHER: _____ SUCCESS? ☐ YES ☐ NO

FAVORITE EUPHEMISM FOR PERFORMING #1:

FAVORITE RESTROOM GRAFFITI OR YOUR ORIGNAL DOODLE:

FAVORITE EUPHEMISM FOR PERFORMING #2:

WHILE YOU WERE HERE, DID YOU:
- ☐ TEXT SOMEONE
- ☐ MAKE A PHONE CALL
- ☐ EMAIL
- ☐ CHECK SOCIAL MEDIA
- ☐ TAKE A SELFIE
- ☐ LOOK IN THE MEDICINE CABINET
- ☐ CHECK YOUR TEETH
- ☐ CHECK OUT YOUR BUTT
- ☐ CHECK YOUR FLY
- ☐ READ
- ☐ FIX YOUR HAIR
- ☐ TAKE SOME EXTRA "ME TIME"
- ☐ TALK TO YOURSELF
- ☐ CONDUCT BUSINESS OTHER THAN YOUR "BUSINESS." CARE TO SHARE?
  _____

FAVORITE NAME FOR THIS ROOM:
- ☐ BATHROOM
- ☐ TOILET
- ☐ POWDER ROOM
- ☐ LAVATORY
- ☐ SHITTER
- ☐ LOO
- ☐ LITTLE GIRLS ROOM
- ☐ LITTLE BOYS ROOM
- ☐ COMFORT STATION
- ☐ OTHER: _____

- ☐ JOHN
- ☐ CAN
- ☐ HEAD
- ☐ POTTY
- ☐ CRAPPER
- ☐ WC

RATINGS:

	1	2	3	4	5
CLEANLINESS	☆	☆	☆	☆	☆
AMBIENCE	☆	☆	☆	☆	☆
AMENITIES	☆	☆	☆	☆	☆
SOUND PROOFING	☆	☆	☆	☆	☆
QUALITY OF THE FLUSH	☆	☆	☆	☆	☆
TOILET PAPER	☆	☆	☆	☆	☆

OVERALL EXPERIENCE:
- ☐ BEST SEAT IN THE HOUSE   ★ ★ ★ ★ ★
- ☐ WOULD POOP HERE AGAIN   ★ ★ ★ ★
- ☐ SHIT GOT REAL   ★ ★ ★
- ☐ SAME SHIT DIFFERENT HOUSE   ★ ★
- ☐ THINGS JUST DIDN'T COME OUT RIGHT   ★

THOUGHTS/MESSAGES: _____
_____
_____

Welcome! PLEASE SEAT YOURSELF AND ENJOY YOUR VISIT!

NAME: _____ DATE: _____ TIME: _____ DURATION OF VISIT: _____
HRS   MIN   SEC

PURPOSE FOR VISIT: 🧻 #1 🧻 #2 🧻 OTHER: _____ SUCCESS? 🧻 YES 🧻 NO

FAVORITE EUPHEMISM FOR PERFORMING #1:

FAVORITE RESTROOM GRAFFITI OR YOUR ORIGNAL DOODLE:

FAVORITE EUPHEMISM FOR PERFORMING #2:

WHILE YOU WERE HERE, DID YOU:
- ☐ TEXT SOMEONE
- ☐ MAKE A PHONE CALL
- ☐ EMAIL
- ☐ CHECK SOCIAL MEDIA
- ☐ TAKE A SELFIE
- ☐ LOOK IN THE MEDICINE CABINET
- ☐ CHECK YOUR TEETH
- ☐ CHECK OUT YOUR BUTT
- ☐ CHECK YOUR FLY
- ☐ READ
- ☐ FIX YOUR HAIR
- ☐ TAKE SOME EXTRA "ME TIME"
- ☐ TALK TO YOURSELF
- ☐ CONDUCT BUSINESS OTHER THAN YOUR "BUSINESS." CARE TO SHARE?
  _____

FAVORITE NAME FOR THIS ROOM:
- ☐ BATHROOM
- ☐ TOILET
- ☐ POWDER ROOM
- ☐ LAVATORY
- ☐ SHITTER
- ☐ LOO
- ☐ LITTLE GIRLS ROOM
- ☐ LITTLE BOYS ROOM
- ☐ COMFORT STATION
- ☐ OTHER: _____

- ☐ JOHN
- ☐ CAN
- ☐ HEAD
- ☐ POTTY
- ☐ CRAPPER
- ☐ WC

THOUGHTS/MESSAGES: _____

RATINGS:
	1	2	3	4	5
CLEANLINESS	☆	☆	☆	☆	☆
AMBIENCE	☆	☆	☆	☆	☆
AMENITIES	☆	☆	☆	☆	☆
SOUND PROOFING	☆	☆	☆	☆	☆
QUALITY OF THE FLUSH	☆	☆	☆	☆	☆
TOILET PAPER	☆	☆	☆	☆	☆

OVERALL EXPERIENCE:
- ☐ BEST SEAT IN THE HOUSE ★ ★ ★ ★ ★
- ☐ WOULD POOP HERE AGAIN ★ ★ ★ ★
- ☐ SHIT GOT REAL ★ ★ ★
- ☐ SAME SHIT DIFFERENT HOUSE ★ ★
- ☐ THINGS JUST DIDN'T COME OUT RIGHT ★

Welcome! PLEASE SEAT YOURSELF AND ENJOY YOUR VISIT!

NAME: _____ DATE: _____ TIME: _____ DURATION OF VISIT: _____

HRS   MIN   SEC

PURPOSE FOR VISIT: 🧻 #1 🧻 #2 🧻 OTHER: _____ SUCCESS? 🧻 YES 🧻 NO

FAVORITE EUPHEMISM FOR PERFORMING #1: | FAVORITE RESTROOM GRAFFITI OR YOUR ORIGNAL DOODLE:

FAVORITE EUPHEMISM FOR PERFORMING #2:

WHILE YOU WERE HERE, DID YOU:
- ☐ TEXT SOMEONE
- ☐ MAKE A PHONE CALL
- ☐ EMAIL
- ☐ CHECK SOCIAL MEDIA
- ☐ TAKE A SELFIE
- ☐ LOOK IN THE MEDICINE CABINET
- ☐ CHECK YOUR TEETH
- ☐ CHECK OUT YOUR BUTT
- ☐ CHECK YOUR FLY
- ☐ READ
- ☐ FIX YOUR HAIR
- ☐ TAKE SOME EXTRA "ME TIME"
- ☐ TALK TO YOURSELF
- ☐ CONDUCT BUSINESS OTHER THAN YOUR "BUSINESS." CARE TO SHARE?
_____

FAVORITE NAME FOR THIS ROOM:
- ☐ BATHROOM
- ☐ TOILET
- ☐ POWDER ROOM
- ☐ LAVATORY
- ☐ SHITTER
- ☐ LOO
- ☐ LITTLE GIRLS ROOM
- ☐ LITTLE BOYS ROOM
- ☐ COMFORT STATION
- ☐ OTHER: _____
- ☐ JOHN
- ☐ CAN
- ☐ HEAD
- ☐ POTTY
- ☐ CRAPPER
- ☐ WC

_____

THOUGHTS/MESSAGES: _____
_____
_____

RATINGS:

	1	2	3	4	5
CLEANLINESS	☆	☆	☆	☆	☆
AMBIENCE	☆	☆	☆	☆	☆
AMENITIES	☆	☆	☆	☆	☆
SOUND PROOFING	☆	☆	☆	☆	☆
QUALITY OF THE FLUSH	☆	☆	☆	☆	☆
TOILET PAPER	☆	☆	☆	☆	☆

OVERALL EXPERIENCE:
- ☐ BEST SEAT IN THE HOUSE ★ ★ ★ ★ ★
- ☐ WOULD POOP HERE AGAIN ★ ★ ★ ★
- ☐ SHIT GOT REAL ★ ★ ★
- ☐ SAME SHIT DIFFERENT HOUSE ★ ★
- ☐ THINGS JUST DIDN'T COME OUT RIGHT ★

Welcome! PLEASE SEAT YOURSELF AND ENJOY YOUR VISIT!

NAME: _____ DATE: _____ TIME: _____ DURATION OF VISIT: _____
HRS   MIN   SEC

PURPOSE FOR VISIT: ☐ #1 ☐ #2 ☐ OTHER: _____ SUCCESS? ☐ YES ☐ NO

FAVORITE EUPHEMISM FOR PERFORMING #1: | FAVORITE RESTROOM GRAFFITI OR YOUR ORIGNAL DOODLE:

FAVORITE EUPHEMISM FOR PERFORMING #2:

WHILE YOU WERE HERE, DID YOU:
- ☐ TEXT SOMEONE
- ☐ MAKE A PHONE CALL
- ☐ EMAIL
- ☐ CHECK SOCIAL MEDIA
- ☐ TAKE A SELFIE
- ☐ LOOK IN THE MEDICINE CABINET
- ☐ CHECK YOUR TEETH
- ☐ CHECK OUT YOUR BUTT
- ☐ CHECK YOUR FLY
- ☐ READ
- ☐ FIX YOUR HAIR
- ☐ TAKE SOME EXTRA "ME TIME"
- ☐ TALK TO YOURSELF
- ☐ CONDUCT BUSINESS OTHER THAN YOUR "BUSINESS." CARE TO SHARE?
_____

FAVORITE NAME FOR THIS ROOM:
- ☐ BATHROOM
- ☐ TOILET
- ☐ POWDER ROOM
- ☐ LAVATORY
- ☐ SHITTER
- ☐ LOO
- ☐ LITTLE GIRLS ROOM
- ☐ LITTLE BOYS ROOM
- ☐ COMFORT STATION
- ☐ OTHER: _____

- ☐ JOHN
- ☐ CAN
- ☐ HEAD
- ☐ POTTY
- ☐ CRAPPER
- ☐ WC

_____

RATINGS:
	1	2	3	4	5
CLEANLINESS	☆	☆	☆	☆	☆
AMBIENCE	☆	☆	☆	☆	☆
AMENITIES	☆	☆	☆	☆	☆
SOUND PROOFING	☆	☆	☆	☆	☆
QUALITY OF THE FLUSH	☆	☆	☆	☆	☆
TOILET PAPER	☆	☆	☆	☆	☆

OVERALL EXPERIENCE:
- ☐ BEST SEAT IN THE HOUSE ★★★★★
- ☐ WOULD POOP HERE AGAIN ★★★★
- ☐ SHIT GOT REAL ★★★
- ☐ SAME SHIT DIFFERENT HOUSE ★★
- ☐ THINGS JUST DIDN'T COME OUT RIGHT ★

THOUGHTS/MESSAGES: _____
_____
_____

Welcome! PLEASE SEAT YOURSELF AND ENJOY YOUR VISIT!

NAME: _____ DATE: _____ TIME: _____ DURATION OF VISIT: _____
HRS   MIN   SEC

PURPOSE FOR VISIT: ⬜ #1   ⬜ #2   ⬜ OTHER: _____   SUCCESS? ⬜ YES ⬜ NO

FAVORITE EUPHEMISM FOR PERFORMING #1:

FAVORITE RESTROOM GRAFFITI OR YOUR ORIGNAL DOODLE:

FAVORITE EUPHEMISM FOR PERFORMING #2:

WHILE YOU WERE HERE, DID YOU:
- ☐ TEXT SOMEONE
- ☐ MAKE A PHONE CALL
- ☐ EMAIL
- ☐ CHECK SOCIAL MEDIA
- ☐ TAKE A SELFIE
- ☐ LOOK IN THE MEDICINE CABINET
- ☐ CHECK YOUR TEETH
- ☐ CHECK OUT YOUR BUTT
- ☐ CHECK YOUR FLY
- ☐ READ
- ☐ FIX YOUR HAIR
- ☐ TAKE SOME EXTRA "ME TIME"
- ☐ TALK TO YOURSELF
- ☐ CONDUCT BUSINESS OTHER THAN YOUR "BUSINESS." CARE TO SHARE?
_____

FAVORITE NAME FOR THIS ROOM:
- ☐ BATHROOM
- ☐ TOILET
- ☐ POWDER ROOM
- ☐ LAVATORY
- ☐ SHITTER
- ☐ LOO
- ☐ LITTLE GIRLS ROOM
- ☐ LITTLE BOYS ROOM
- ☐ COMFORT STATION
- ☐ OTHER: _____

- ☐ JOHN
- ☐ CAN
- ☐ HEAD
- ☐ POTTY
- ☐ CRAPPER
- ☐ WC

_____

RATINGS:

	1	2	3	4	5
CLEANLINESS	☆	☆	☆	☆	☆
AMBIENCE	☆	☆	☆	☆	☆
AMENITIES	☆	☆	☆	☆	☆
SOUND PROOFING	☆	☆	☆	☆	☆
QUALITY OF THE FLUSH	☆	☆	☆	☆	☆
TOILET PAPER	☆	☆	☆	☆	☆

OVERALL EXPERIENCE:
- ☐ BEST SEAT IN THE HOUSE ★ ★ ★ ★ ★
- ☐ WOULD POOP HERE AGAIN ★ ★ ★ ★
- ☐ SHIT GOT REAL ★ ★ ★
- ☐ SAME SHIT DIFFERENT HOUSE ★ ★
- ☐ THINGS JUST DIDN'T COME OUT RIGHT ★

THOUGHTS/MESSAGES: _____
_____
_____

Welcome! PLEASE SEAT YOURSELF AND ENJOY YOUR VISIT!

NAME: _____ DATE: _____ TIME: _____ DURATION OF VISIT: _____
                                                                              HRS   MIN   SEC

PURPOSE FOR VISIT: 🧻 #1 🧻 #2 🧻 OTHER: _____ SUCCESS? 🧻 YES 🧻 NO

FAVORITE EUPHEMISM FOR PERFORMING #1:

FAVORITE RESTROOM GRAFFITI OR YOUR ORIGNAL DOODLE:

FAVORITE EUPHEMISM FOR PERFORMING #2:

WHILE YOU WERE HERE, DID YOU:
- ☐ TEXT SOMEONE
- ☐ MAKE A PHONE CALL
- ☐ EMAIL
- ☐ CHECK SOCIAL MEDIA
- ☐ TAKE A SELFIE
- ☐ LOOK IN THE MEDICINE CABINET
- ☐ CHECK YOUR TEETH
- ☐ CHECK OUT YOUR BUTT
- ☐ CHECK YOUR FLY
- ☐ READ
- ☐ FIX YOUR HAIR
- ☐ TAKE SOME EXTRA "ME TIME"
- ☐ TALK TO YOURSELF
- ☐ CONDUCT BUSINESS OTHER THAN YOUR "BUSINESS." CARE TO SHARE?
_____

FAVORITE NAME FOR THIS ROOM:
- ☐ BATHROOM
- ☐ TOILET
- ☐ POWDER ROOM
- ☐ LAVATORY
- ☐ SHITTER
- ☐ LOO
- ☐ LITTLE GIRLS ROOM
- ☐ LITTLE BOYS ROOM
- ☐ COMFORT STATION
- ☐ OTHER: _____

- ☐ JOHN
- ☐ CAN
- ☐ HEAD
- ☐ POTTY
- ☐ CRAPPER
- ☐ WC

_____
_____

RATINGS:

	1	2	3	4	5
CLEANLINESS	☆	☆	☆	☆	☆
AMBIENCE	☆	☆	☆	☆	☆
AMENITIES	☆	☆	☆	☆	☆
SOUND PROOFING	☆	☆	☆	☆	☆
QUALITY OF THE FLUSH	☆	☆	☆	☆	☆
TOILET PAPER	☆	☆	☆	☆	☆

OVERALL EXPERIENCE:
- ☐ BEST SEAT IN THE HOUSE ★ ★ ★ ★ ★
- ☐ WOULD POOP HERE AGAIN ★ ★ ★ ★
- ☐ SHIT GOT REAL ★ ★ ★
- ☐ SAME SHIT DIFFERENT HOUSE ★ ★
- ☐ THINGS JUST DIDN'T COME OUT RIGHT ★

THOUGHTS/MESSAGES: _____
_____
_____

Welcome! PLEASE SEAT YOURSELF AND ENJOY YOUR VISIT!

NAME: _____ DATE: _____ TIME: _____ DURATION OF VISIT: _____
HRS MIN SEC

PURPOSE FOR VISIT: 🧻 #1 🧻 #2 🧻 OTHER: _____ SUCCESS? 🧻 YES 🧻 NO

FAVORITE EUPHEMISM FOR PERFORMING #1:

FAVORITE RESTROOM GRAFFITI OR YOUR ORIGNAL DOODLE:

FAVORITE EUPHEMISM FOR PERFORMING #2:

WHILE YOU WERE HERE, DID YOU:
- ☐ TEXT SOMEONE
- ☐ MAKE A PHONE CALL
- ☐ EMAIL
- ☐ CHECK SOCIAL MEDIA
- ☐ TAKE A SELFIE
- ☐ LOOK IN THE MEDICINE CABINET
- ☐ CHECK YOUR TEETH
- ☐ CHECK OUT YOUR BUTT
- ☐ CHECK YOUR FLY
- ☐ READ
- ☐ FIX YOUR HAIR
- ☐ TAKE SOME EXTRA "ME TIME"
- ☐ TALK TO YOURSELF
- ☐ CONDUCT BUSINESS OTHER THAN YOUR "BUSINESS." CARE TO SHARE?
_____

FAVORITE NAME FOR THIS ROOM:
- ☐ BATHROOM
- ☐ TOILET
- ☐ POWDER ROOM
- ☐ LAVATORY
- ☐ SHITTER
- ☐ LOO
- ☐ LITTLE GIRLS ROOM
- ☐ LITTLE BOYS ROOM
- ☐ COMFORT STATION
- ☐ OTHER: _____
- ☐ JOHN
- ☐ CAN
- ☐ HEAD
- ☐ POTTY
- ☐ CRAPPER
- ☐ WC

_____

THOUGHTS/MESSAGES: _____
_____
_____

RATINGS:

	1 2 3 4 5
CLEANLINESS	☆ ☆ ☆ ☆ ☆
AMBIENCE	☆ ☆ ☆ ☆ ☆
AMENITIES	☆ ☆ ☆ ☆ ☆
SOUND PROOFING	☆ ☆ ☆ ☆ ☆
QUALITY OF THE FLUSH	☆ ☆ ☆ ☆ ☆
TOILET PAPER	☆ ☆ ☆ ☆ ☆

OVERALL EXPERIENCE:
- ☐ BEST SEAT IN THE HOUSE ★ ★ ★ ★ ★
- ☐ WOULD POOP HERE AGAIN ★ ★ ★ ★
- ☐ SHIT GOT REAL ★ ★ ★
- ☐ SAME SHIT DIFFERENT HOUSE ★ ★
- ☐ THINGS JUST DIDN'T COME OUT RIGHT ★

Welcome! PLEASE SEAT YOURSELF AND ENJOY YOUR VISIT!

NAME: _____ DATE: _____ TIME: _____ DURATION OF VISIT: _____
HRS   MIN   SEC

PURPOSE FOR VISIT: ▢ #1 ▢ #2 ▢ OTHER: _____ SUCCESS? ▢ YES ▢ NO

FAVORITE EUPHEMISM FOR PERFORMING #1:   FAVORITE RESTROOM GRAFFITI OR YOUR ORIGNAL DOODLE:

FAVORITE EUPHEMISM FOR PERFORMING #2:

WHILE YOU WERE HERE, DID YOU:
☐ TEXT SOMEONE
☐ MAKE A PHONE CALL
☐ EMAIL
☐ CHECK SOCIAL MEDIA
☐ TAKE A SELFIE
☐ LOOK IN THE MEDICINE CABINET
☐ CHECK YOUR TEETH
☐ CHECK OUT YOUR BUTT
☐ CHECK YOUR FLY
☐ READ
☐ FIX YOUR HAIR
☐ TAKE SOME EXTRA "ME TIME"
☐ TALK TO YOURSELF
☐ CONDUCT BUSINESS OTHER THAN YOUR "BUSINESS." CARE TO SHARE?
_____

FAVORITE NAME FOR THIS ROOM:
☐ BATHROOM   ☐ JOHN
☐ TOILET   ☐ CAN
☐ POWDER ROOM   ☐ HEAD
☐ LAVATORY   ☐ POTTY
☐ SHITTER   ☐ CRAPPER
☐ LOO   ☐ WC
☐ LITTLE GIRLS ROOM
☐ LITTLE BOYS ROOM
☐ COMFORT STATION
☐ OTHER: _____
_____

THOUGHTS/MESSAGES: _____
_____
_____

RATINGS: 1 2 3 4 5
CLEANLINESS   ☆ ☆ ☆ ☆ ☆
AMBIENCE   ☆ ☆ ☆ ☆ ☆
AMENITIES   ☆ ☆ ☆ ☆ ☆
SOUND PROOFING   ☆ ☆ ☆ ☆ ☆
QUALITY OF THE FLUSH ☆ ☆ ☆ ☆ ☆
TOILET PAPER   ☆ ☆ ☆ ☆ ☆

OVERALL EXPERIENCE:
☐ BEST SEAT IN THE HOUSE   ★ ★ ★ ★ ★
☐ WOULD POOP HERE AGAIN   ★ ★ ★ ★
☐ SHIT GOT REAL   ★ ★ ★
☐ SAME SHIT DIFFERENT HOUSE   ★ ★
☐ THINGS JUST DIDN'T COME OUT RIGHT ★

Welcome! PLEASE SEAT YOURSELF AND ENJOY YOUR VISIT!

NAME: _____ DATE: _____ TIME: _____ DURATION OF VISIT: _____
                                                                                          HRS   MIN   SEC

PURPOSE FOR VISIT: #1   #2   OTHER: _____   SUCCESS? ☐ YES ☐ NO

FAVORITE EUPHEMISM FOR PERFORMING #1:   FAVORITE RESTROOM GRAFFITI OR YOUR ORIGNAL DOODLE:

FAVORITE EUPHEMISM FOR PERFORMING #2:

WHILE YOU WERE HERE, DID YOU:
- ☐ TEXT SOMEONE
- ☐ MAKE A PHONE CALL
- ☐ EMAIL
- ☐ CHECK SOCIAL MEDIA
- ☐ TAKE A SELFIE
- ☐ LOOK IN THE MEDICINE CABINET
- ☐ CHECK YOUR TEETH
- ☐ CHECK OUT YOUR BUTT
- ☐ CHECK YOUR FLY
- ☐ READ
- ☐ FIX YOUR HAIR
- ☐ TAKE SOME EXTRA "ME TIME"
- ☐ TALK TO YOURSELF
- ☐ CONDUCT BUSINESS OTHER THAN YOUR "BUSINESS." CARE TO SHARE?
  _____

FAVORITE NAME FOR THIS ROOM:
- ☐ BATHROOM
- ☐ TOILET
- ☐ POWDER ROOM
- ☐ LAVATORY
- ☐ SHITTER
- ☐ LOO
- ☐ LITTLE GIRLS ROOM
- ☐ LITTLE BOYS ROOM
- ☐ COMFORT STATION
- ☐ OTHER: _____
- ☐ JOHN
- ☐ CAN
- ☐ HEAD
- ☐ POTTY
- ☐ CRAPPER
- ☐ WC

_____

THOUGHTS/MESSAGES: _____
_____
_____

RATINGS: 1 2 3 4 5
- CLEANLINESS   ☆ ☆ ☆ ☆ ☆
- AMBIENCE   ☆ ☆ ☆ ☆ ☆
- AMENITIES   ☆ ☆ ☆ ☆ ☆
- SOUND PROOFING   ☆ ☆ ☆ ☆ ☆
- QUALITY OF THE FLUSH ☆ ☆ ☆ ☆ ☆
- TOILET PAPER   ☆ ☆ ☆ ☆ ☆

OVERALL EXPERIENCE:
- ☐ BEST SEAT IN THE HOUSE   ★ ★ ★ ★ ★
- ☐ WOULD POOP HERE AGAIN   ★ ★ ★ ★
- ☐ SHIT GOT REAL   ★ ★ ★
- ☐ SAME SHIT DIFFERENT HOUSE   ★ ★
- ☐ THINGS JUST DIDN'T COME OUT RIGHT   ★

Welcome! PLEASE SEAT YOURSELF AND ENJOY YOUR VISIT!

NAME: _____ DATE: _____ TIME: _____ DURATION OF VISIT: _____
HRS   MIN   SEC

PURPOSE FOR VISIT: ☐ #1 ☐ #2 ☐ OTHER: _____ SUCCESS? ☐ YES ☐ NO

FAVORITE EUPHEMISM FOR PERFORMING #1:

FAVORITE RESTROOM GRAFFITI OR YOUR ORIGNAL DOODLE:

FAVORITE EUPHEMISM FOR PERFORMING #2:

WHILE YOU WERE HERE, DID YOU:
☐ TEXT SOMEONE
☐ MAKE A PHONE CALL
☐ EMAIL
☐ CHECK SOCIAL MEDIA
☐ TAKE A SELFIE
☐ LOOK IN THE MEDICINE CABINET
☐ CHECK YOUR TEETH
☐ CHECK OUT YOUR BUTT
☐ CHECK YOUR FLY
☐ READ
☐ FIX YOUR HAIR
☐ TAKE SOME EXTRA "ME TIME"
☐ TALK TO YOURSELF
☐ CONDUCT BUSINESS OTHER THAN YOUR "BUSINESS." CARE TO SHARE?
_____

FAVORITE NAME FOR THIS ROOM:
☐ BATHROOM   ☐ JOHN
☐ TOILET   ☐ CAN
☐ POWDER ROOM   ☐ HEAD
☐ LAVATORY   ☐ POTTY
☐ SHITTER   ☐ CRAPPER
☐ LOO   ☐ WC
☐ LITTLE GIRLS ROOM
☐ LITTLE BOYS ROOM
☐ COMFORT STATION
☐ OTHER: _____

THOUGHTS/MESSAGES: _____
_____
_____

RATINGS:
	1	2	3	4	5
CLEANLINESS	☆	☆	☆	☆	☆
AMBIENCE	☆	☆	☆	☆	☆
AMENITIES	☆	☆	☆	☆	☆
SOUND PROOFING	☆	☆	☆	☆	☆
QUALITY OF THE FLUSH	☆	☆	☆	☆	☆
TOILET PAPER	☆	☆	☆	☆	☆

OVERALL EXPERIENCE:
☐ BEST SEAT IN THE HOUSE ★★★★★
☐ WOULD POOP HERE AGAIN ★★★★
☐ SHIT GOT REAL ★★★
☐ SAME SHIT DIFFERENT HOUSE ★★
☐ THINGS JUST DIDN'T COME OUT RIGHT ★

Welcome! PLEASE SEAT YOURSELF AND ENJOY YOUR VISIT!

NAME: _____ DATE: _____ TIME: _____ DURATION OF VISIT: _____
HRS   MIN   SEC

PURPOSE FOR VISIT: ☐ #1 ☐ #2 ☐ OTHER: _____ SUCCESS? ☐ YES ☐ NO

FAVORITE EUPHEMISM FOR PERFORMING #1:

FAVORITE RESTROOM GRAFFITI OR YOUR ORIGNAL DOODLE:

FAVORITE EUPHEMISM FOR PERFORMING #2:

WHILE YOU WERE HERE, DID YOU:
- ☐ TEXT SOMEONE
- ☐ MAKE A PHONE CALL
- ☐ EMAIL
- ☐ CHECK SOCIAL MEDIA
- ☐ TAKE A SELFIE
- ☐ LOOK IN THE MEDICINE CABINET
- ☐ CHECK YOUR TEETH
- ☐ CHECK OUT YOUR BUTT
- ☐ CHECK YOUR FLY
- ☐ READ
- ☐ FIX YOUR HAIR
- ☐ TAKE SOME EXTRA "ME TIME"
- ☐ TALK TO YOURSELF
- ☐ CONDUCT BUSINESS OTHER THAN YOUR "BUSINESS." CARE TO SHARE?

FAVORITE NAME FOR THIS ROOM:
- ☐ BATHROOM
- ☐ TOILET
- ☐ POWDER ROOM
- ☐ LAVATORY
- ☐ SHITTER
- ☐ LOO
- ☐ LITTLE GIRLS ROOM
- ☐ LITTLE BOYS ROOM
- ☐ COMFORT STATION
- ☐ OTHER: _____
- ☐ JOHN
- ☐ CAN
- ☐ HEAD
- ☐ POTTY
- ☐ CRAPPER
- ☐ WC

THOUGHTS/MESSAGES: _____

RATINGS:

	1	2	3	4	5
CLEANLINESS	☆	☆	☆	☆	☆
AMBIENCE	☆	☆	☆	☆	☆
AMENITIES	☆	☆	☆	☆	☆
SOUND PROOFING	☆	☆	☆	☆	☆
QUALITY OF THE FLUSH	☆	☆	☆	☆	☆
TOILET PAPER	☆	☆	☆	☆	☆

OVERALL EXPERIENCE:
- ☐ BEST SEAT IN THE HOUSE ★ ★ ★ ★ ★
- ☐ WOULD POOP HERE AGAIN ★ ★ ★ ★
- ☐ SHIT GOT REAL ★ ★ ★
- ☐ SAME SHIT DIFFERENT HOUSE ★ ★
- ☐ THINGS JUST DIDN'T COME OUT RIGHT ★

Welcome! PLEASE SEAT YOURSELF AND ENJOY YOUR VISIT!

NAME: _____ DATE: _____ TIME: _____ DURATION OF VISIT: _____
HRS   MIN   SEC

PURPOSE FOR VISIT: 🧻 #1 🧻 #2 🧻 OTHER: _____ SUCCESS? 🧻 YES 🧻 NO

FAVORITE EUPHEMISM FOR PERFORMING #1:

FAVORITE RESTROOM GRAFFITI OR YOUR ORIGNAL DOODLE:

FAVORITE EUPHEMISM FOR PERFORMING #2:

WHILE YOU WERE HERE, DID YOU:
- ☐ TEXT SOMEONE
- ☐ MAKE A PHONE CALL
- ☐ EMAIL
- ☐ CHECK SOCIAL MEDIA
- ☐ TAKE A SELFIE
- ☐ LOOK IN THE MEDICINE CABINET
- ☐ CHECK YOUR TEETH
- ☐ CHECK OUT YOUR BUTT
- ☐ CHECK YOUR FLY
- ☐ READ
- ☐ FIX YOUR HAIR
- ☐ TAKE SOME EXTRA "ME TIME"
- ☐ TALK TO YOURSELF
- ☐ CONDUCT BUSINESS OTHER THAN YOUR "BUSINESS." CARE TO SHARE?
_____

FAVORITE NAME FOR THIS ROOM:
- ☐ BATHROOM
- ☐ TOILET
- ☐ POWDER ROOM
- ☐ LAVATORY
- ☐ SHITTER
- ☐ LOO
- ☐ LITTLE GIRLS ROOM
- ☐ LITTLE BOYS ROOM
- ☐ COMFORT STATION
- ☐ OTHER: _____

- ☐ JOHN
- ☐ CAN
- ☐ HEAD
- ☐ POTTY
- ☐ CRAPPER
- ☐ WC

_____

THOUGHTS/MESSAGES: _____
_____
_____

RATINGS:
	1 2 3 4 5
CLEANLINESS	☆ ☆ ☆ ☆ ☆
AMBIENCE	☆ ☆ ☆ ☆ ☆
AMENITIES	☆ ☆ ☆ ☆ ☆
SOUND PROOFING	☆ ☆ ☆ ☆ ☆
QUALITY OF THE FLUSH	☆ ☆ ☆ ☆ ☆
TOILET PAPER	☆ ☆ ☆ ☆ ☆

OVERALL EXPERIENCE:
- ☐ BEST SEAT IN THE HOUSE ★ ★ ★ ★ ★
- ☐ WOULD POOP HERE AGAIN ★ ★ ★ ★
- ☐ SHIT GOT REAL ★ ★ ★
- ☐ SAME SHIT DIFFERENT HOUSE ★ ★
- ☐ THINGS JUST DIDN'T COME OUT RIGHT ★

Welcome! PLEASE SEAT YOURSELF AND ENJOY YOUR VISIT!

NAME: _____ DATE: _____ TIME: _____ DURATION OF VISIT: _____
HRS   MIN   SEC

PURPOSE FOR VISIT: ▢ #1 ▢ #2 ▢ OTHER: _____ SUCCESS? ▢ YES ▢ NO

FAVORITE EUPHEMISM FOR PERFORMING #1: _____

FAVORITE RESTROOM GRAFFITI OR YOUR ORIGNAL DOODLE:

FAVORITE EUPHEMISM FOR PERFORMING #2: _____

WHILE YOU WERE HERE, DID YOU:
- ☐ TEXT SOMEONE
- ☐ MAKE A PHONE CALL
- ☐ EMAIL
- ☐ CHECK SOCIAL MEDIA
- ☐ TAKE A SELFIE
- ☐ LOOK IN THE MEDICINE CABINET
- ☐ CHECK YOUR TEETH
- ☐ CHECK OUT YOUR BUTT
- ☐ CHECK YOUR FLY
- ☐ READ
- ☐ FIX YOUR HAIR
- ☐ TAKE SOME EXTRA "ME TIME"
- ☐ TALK TO YOURSELF
- ☐ CONDUCT BUSINESS OTHER THAN YOUR "BUSINESS." CARE TO SHARE?
_____

FAVORITE NAME FOR THIS ROOM:
- ☐ BATHROOM
- ☐ TOILET
- ☐ POWDER ROOM
- ☐ LAVATORY
- ☐ SHITTER
- ☐ LOO
- ☐ LITTLE GIRLS ROOM
- ☐ LITTLE BOYS ROOM
- ☐ COMFORT STATION
- ☐ OTHER: _____
- ☐ JOHN
- ☐ CAN
- ☐ HEAD
- ☐ POTTY
- ☐ CRAPPER
- ☐ WC

RATINGS:

	1	2	3	4	5
CLEANLINESS	☆	☆	☆	☆	☆
AMBIENCE	☆	☆	☆	☆	☆
AMENITIES	☆	☆	☆	☆	☆
SOUND PROOFING	☆	☆	☆	☆	☆
QUALITY OF THE FLUSH	☆	☆	☆	☆	☆
TOILET PAPER	☆	☆	☆	☆	☆

OVERALL EXPERIENCE:
- ☐ BEST SEAT IN THE HOUSE ★ ★ ★ ★ ★
- ☐ WOULD POOP HERE AGAIN ★ ★ ★ ★
- ☐ SHIT GOT REAL ★ ★ ★
- ☐ SAME SHIT DIFFERENT HOUSE ★ ★
- ☐ THINGS JUST DIDN'T COME OUT RIGHT ★

THOUGHTS/MESSAGES: _____
_____
_____

Welcome! PLEASE SEAT YOURSELF AND ENJOY YOUR VISIT!

NAME: _____ DATE: _____ TIME: _____ DURATION OF VISIT: _____
HRS   MIN   SEC

PURPOSE FOR VISIT: ☐ #1 ☐ #2 ☐ OTHER: _____ SUCCESS? ☐ YES ☐ NO

FAVORITE EUPHEMISM FOR PERFORMING #1:

FAVORITE RESTROOM GRAFFITI OR YOUR ORIGNAL DOODLE:

FAVORITE EUPHEMISM FOR PERFORMING #2:

WHILE YOU WERE HERE, DID YOU:
☐ TEXT SOMEONE
☐ MAKE A PHONE CALL
☐ EMAIL
☐ CHECK SOCIAL MEDIA
☐ TAKE A SELFIE
☐ LOOK IN THE MEDICINE CABINET
☐ CHECK YOUR TEETH
☐ CHECK OUT YOUR BUTT
☐ CHECK YOUR FLY
☐ READ
☐ FIX YOUR HAIR
☐ TAKE SOME EXTRA "ME TIME"
☐ TALK TO YOURSELF
☐ CONDUCT BUSINESS OTHER THAN YOUR "BUSINESS." CARE TO SHARE?
_____

FAVORITE NAME FOR THIS ROOM:
☐ BATHROOM   ☐ JOHN
☐ TOILET   ☐ CAN
☐ POWDER ROOM   ☐ HEAD
☐ LAVATORY   ☐ POTTY
☐ SHITTER   ☐ CRAPPER
☐ LOO   ☐ WC
☐ LITTLE GIRLS ROOM
☐ LITTLE BOYS ROOM
☐ COMFORT STATION
☐ OTHER: _____
_____

THOUGHTS/MESSAGES: _____
_____
_____

RATINGS: 1 2 3 4 5
CLEANLINESS   ☆ ☆ ☆ ☆ ☆
AMBIENCE   ☆ ☆ ☆ ☆ ☆
AMENITIES   ☆ ☆ ☆ ☆ ☆
SOUND PROOFING   ☆ ☆ ☆ ☆ ☆
QUALITY OF THE FLUSH ☆ ☆ ☆ ☆ ☆
TOILET PAPER   ☆ ☆ ☆ ☆ ☆

OVERALL EXPERIENCE:
☐ BEST SEAT IN THE HOUSE   ★ ★ ★ ★ ★
☐ WOULD POOP HERE AGAIN   ★ ★ ★ ★
☐ SHIT GOT REAL   ★ ★ ★
☐ SAME SHIT DIFFERENT HOUSE   ★ ★
☐ THINGS JUST DIDN'T COME OUT RIGHT   ★

Welcome! PLEASE SEAT YOURSELF AND ENJOY YOUR VISIT!

NAME: _____ DATE: _____ TIME: _____ DURATION OF VISIT: _____
HRS   MIN   SEC

PURPOSE FOR VISIT: ☐ #1 ☐ #2 ☐ OTHER: _____   SUCCESS? ☐ YES ☐ NO

FAVORITE EUPHEMISM FOR PERFORMING #1:

FAVORITE RESTROOM GRAFFITI OR YOUR ORIGNAL DOODLE:

FAVORITE EUPHEMISM FOR PERFORMING #2:

WHILE YOU WERE HERE, DID YOU:
- ☐ TEXT SOMEONE
- ☐ MAKE A PHONE CALL
- ☐ EMAIL
- ☐ CHECK SOCIAL MEDIA
- ☐ TAKE A SELFIE
- ☐ LOOK IN THE MEDICINE CABINET
- ☐ CHECK YOUR TEETH
- ☐ CHECK OUT YOUR BUTT
- ☐ CHECK YOUR FLY
- ☐ READ
- ☐ FIX YOUR HAIR
- ☐ TAKE SOME EXTRA "ME TIME"
- ☐ TALK TO YOURSELF
- ☐ CONDUCT BUSINESS OTHER THAN YOUR "BUSINESS." CARE TO SHARE?
_____

FAVORITE NAME FOR THIS ROOM:
- ☐ BATHROOM
- ☐ TOILET
- ☐ POWDER ROOM
- ☐ LAVATORY
- ☐ SHITTER
- ☐ LOO
- ☐ LITTLE GIRLS ROOM
- ☐ LITTLE BOYS ROOM
- ☐ COMFORT STATION
- ☐ OTHER: _____
- ☐ JOHN
- ☐ CAN
- ☐ HEAD
- ☐ POTTY
- ☐ CRAPPER
- ☐ WC

_____

THOUGHTS/MESSAGES: _____
_____
_____

RATINGS: 1 2 3 4 5
CLEANLINESS   ☆ ☆ ☆ ☆ ☆
AMBIENCE   ☆ ☆ ☆ ☆ ☆
AMENITIES   ☆ ☆ ☆ ☆ ☆
SOUND PROOFING   ☆ ☆ ☆ ☆ ☆
QUALITY OF THE FLUSH ☆ ☆ ☆ ☆ ☆
TOILET PAPER   ☆ ☆ ☆ ☆ ☆

OVERALL EXPERIENCE:
- ☐ BEST SEAT IN THE HOUSE   ★ ★ ★ ★ ★
- ☐ WOULD POOP HERE AGAIN   ★ ★ ★ ★
- ☐ SHIT GOT REAL   ★ ★ ★
- ☐ SAME SHIT DIFFERENT HOUSE   ★ ★
- ☐ THINGS JUST DIDN'T COME OUT RIGHT ★

Welcome! PLEASE SEAT YOURSELF AND ENJOY YOUR VISIT!

NAME: _____ DATE: _____ TIME: _____ DURATION OF VISIT: _____
HRS   MIN   SEC

PURPOSE FOR VISIT: ▢ #1 ▢ #2 ▢ OTHER: _____ SUCCESS? ▢ YES ▢ NO

FAVORITE EUPHEMISM FOR PERFORMING #1:

FAVORITE RESTROOM GRAFFITI OR YOUR ORIGNAL DOODLE:

FAVORITE EUPHEMISM FOR PERFORMING #2:

WHILE YOU WERE HERE, DID YOU:
☐ TEXT SOMEONE
☐ MAKE A PHONE CALL
☐ EMAIL
☐ CHECK SOCIAL MEDIA
☐ TAKE A SELFIE
☐ LOOK IN THE MEDICINE CABINET
☐ CHECK YOUR TEETH
☐ CHECK OUT YOUR BUTT
☐ CHECK YOUR FLY
☐ READ
☐ FIX YOUR HAIR
☐ TAKE SOME EXTRA "ME TIME"
☐ TALK TO YOURSELF
☐ CONDUCT BUSINESS OTHER THAN
  YOUR "BUSINESS." CARE TO SHARE?
_____

FAVORITE NAME FOR THIS ROOM:
☐ BATHROOM   ☐ JOHN
☐ TOILET   ☐ CAN
☐ POWDER ROOM   ☐ HEAD
☐ LAVATORY   ☐ POTTY
☐ SHITTER   ☐ CRAPPER
☐ LOO   ☐ WC
☐ LITTLE GIRLS ROOM
☐ LITTLE BOYS ROOM
☐ COMFORT STATION
☐ OTHER: _____
_____

THOUGHTS/MESSAGES: _____
_____
_____

RATINGS:
	1 2 3 4 5
CLEANLINESS	☆ ☆ ☆ ☆ ☆
AMBIENCE	☆ ☆ ☆ ☆ ☆
AMENITIES	☆ ☆ ☆ ☆ ☆
SOUND PROOFING	☆ ☆ ☆ ☆ ☆
QUALITY OF THE FLUSH	☆ ☆ ☆ ☆ ☆
TOILET PAPER	☆ ☆ ☆ ☆ ☆

OVERALL EXPERIENCE:
☐ BEST SEAT IN THE HOUSE ★ ★ ★ ★ ★
☐ WOULD POOP HERE AGAIN ★ ★ ★ ★
☐ SHIT GOT REAL ★ ★ ★
☐ SAME SHIT DIFFERENT HOUSE ★ ★
☐ THINGS JUST DIDN'T COME OUT RIGHT ★

Welcome! PLEASE SEAT YOURSELF AND ENJOY YOUR VISIT!

NAME: _____ DATE: _____ TIME: _____ DURATION OF VISIT: _____
                                                                                    HRS   MIN   SEC

PURPOSE FOR VISIT: ☐ #1 ☐ #2 ☐ OTHER: _____ SUCCESS? ☐ YES ☐ NO

FAVORITE EUPHEMISM FOR PERFORMING #1:

FAVORITE EUPHEMISM FOR PERFORMING #2:

FAVORITE RESTROOM GRAFFITI OR YOUR ORIGNAL DOODLE:

WHILE YOU WERE HERE, DID YOU:
- ☐ TEXT SOMEONE
- ☐ MAKE A PHONE CALL
- ☐ EMAIL
- ☐ CHECK SOCIAL MEDIA
- ☐ TAKE A SELFIE
- ☐ LOOK IN THE MEDICINE CABINET
- ☐ CHECK YOUR TEETH
- ☐ CHECK OUT YOUR BUTT
- ☐ CHECK YOUR FLY
- ☐ READ
- ☐ FIX YOUR HAIR
- ☐ TAKE SOME EXTRA "ME TIME"
- ☐ TALK TO YOURSELF
- ☐ CONDUCT BUSINESS OTHER THAN YOUR "BUSINESS." CARE TO SHARE?
  _____

FAVORITE NAME FOR THIS ROOM:
- ☐ BATHROOM
- ☐ TOILET
- ☐ POWDER ROOM
- ☐ LAVATORY
- ☐ SHITTER
- ☐ LOO
- ☐ LITTLE GIRLS ROOM
- ☐ LITTLE BOYS ROOM
- ☐ COMFORT STATION
- ☐ OTHER: _____
- ☐ JOHN
- ☐ CAN
- ☐ HEAD
- ☐ POTTY
- ☐ CRAPPER
- ☐ WC

_____

THOUGHTS/MESSAGES: _____
_____

RATINGS: 1 2 3 4 5
CLEANLINESS	☆ ☆ ☆ ☆ ☆
AMBIENCE	☆ ☆ ☆ ☆ ☆
AMENITIES	☆ ☆ ☆ ☆ ☆
SOUND PROOFING	☆ ☆ ☆ ☆ ☆
QUALITY OF THE FLUSH	☆ ☆ ☆ ☆ ☆
TOILET PAPER	☆ ☆ ☆ ☆ ☆

OVERALL EXPERIENCE:
- ☐ BEST SEAT IN THE HOUSE ★ ★ ★ ★ ★
- ☐ WOULD POOP HERE AGAIN ★ ★ ★ ★
- ☐ SHIT GOT REAL ★ ★ ★
- ☐ SAME SHIT DIFFERENT HOUSE ★ ★
- ☐ THINGS JUST DIDN'T COME OUT RIGHT ★

NAME: _____ DATE: _____ TIME: _____ DURATION OF VISIT: _____
HRS   MIN   SEC

PURPOSE FOR VISIT: ☐ #1 ☐ #2 ☐ OTHER: _____ SUCCESS? ☐ YES ☐ NO

FAVORITE EUPHEMISM FOR PERFORMING #1:

FAVORITE RESTROOM GRAFFITI OR YOUR ORIGNAL DOODLE:

FAVORITE EUPHEMISM FOR PERFORMING #2:

WHILE YOU WERE HERE, DID YOU:
- ☐ TEXT SOMEONE
- ☐ MAKE A PHONE CALL
- ☐ EMAIL
- ☐ CHECK SOCIAL MEDIA
- ☐ TAKE A SELFIE
- ☐ LOOK IN THE MEDICINE CABINET
- ☐ CHECK YOUR TEETH
- ☐ CHECK OUT YOUR BUTT
- ☐ CHECK YOUR FLY
- ☐ READ
- ☐ FIX YOUR HAIR
- ☐ TAKE SOME EXTRA "ME TIME"
- ☐ TALK TO YOURSELF
- ☐ CONDUCT BUSINESS OTHER THAN YOUR "BUSINESS." CARE TO SHARE?
  _____

FAVORITE NAME FOR THIS ROOM:
- ☐ BATHROOM
- ☐ TOILET
- ☐ POWDER ROOM
- ☐ LAVATORY
- ☐ SHITTER
- ☐ LOO
- ☐ LITTLE GIRLS ROOM
- ☐ LITTLE BOYS ROOM
- ☐ COMFORT STATION
- ☐ OTHER: _____
- ☐ JOHN
- ☐ CAN
- ☐ HEAD
- ☐ POTTY
- ☐ CRAPPER
- ☐ WC

_____

RATINGS:	1	2	3	4	5
CLEANLINESS	☆	☆	☆	☆	☆
AMBIENCE	☆	☆	☆	☆	☆
AMENITIES	☆	☆	☆	☆	☆
SOUND PROOFING	☆	☆	☆	☆	☆
QUALITY OF THE FLUSH	☆	☆	☆	☆	☆
TOILET PAPER	☆	☆	☆	☆	☆

OVERALL EXPERIENCE:
- ☐ BEST SEAT IN THE HOUSE ★ ★ ★ ★ ★
- ☐ WOULD POOP HERE AGAIN ★ ★ ★ ★
- ☐ SHIT GOT REAL ★ ★ ★
- ☐ SAME SHIT DIFFERENT HOUSE ★ ★
- ☐ THINGS JUST DIDN'T COME OUT RIGHT ★

THOUGHTS/MESSAGES: _____
_____
_____

Welcome! PLEASE SEAT YOURSELF AND ENJOY YOUR VISIT!

NAME: _____ DATE: _____ TIME: _____ DURATION OF VISIT: _____
HRS   MIN   SEC

PURPOSE FOR VISIT: ☐ #1 ☐ #2 ☐ OTHER: _____ SUCCESS? ☐ YES ☐ NO

FAVORITE EUPHEMISM FOR PERFORMING #1:

FAVORITE RESTROOM GRAFFITI OR YOUR ORIGNAL DOODLE:

FAVORITE EUPHEMISM FOR PERFORMING #2:

WHILE YOU WERE HERE, DID YOU:
☐ TEXT SOMEONE
☐ MAKE A PHONE CALL
☐ EMAIL
☐ CHECK SOCIAL MEDIA
☐ TAKE A SELFIE
☐ LOOK IN THE MEDICINE CABINET
☐ CHECK YOUR TEETH
☐ CHECK OUT YOUR BUTT
☐ CHECK YOUR FLY
☐ READ
☐ FIX YOUR HAIR
☐ TAKE SOME EXTRA "ME TIME"
☐ TALK TO YOURSELF
☐ CONDUCT BUSINESS OTHER THAN
YOUR "BUSINESS." CARE TO SHARE?
_____

FAVORITE NAME FOR THIS ROOM:
☐ BATHROOM   ☐ JOHN
☐ TOILET   ☐ CAN
☐ POWDER ROOM   ☐ HEAD
☐ LAVATORY   ☐ POTTY
☐ SHITTER   ☐ CRAPPER
☐ LOO   ☐ WC
☐ LITTLE GIRLS ROOM
☐ LITTLE BOYS ROOM
☐ COMFORT STATION
☐ OTHER: _____

_____

RATINGS: 1 2 3 4 5
CLEANLINESS   ☆ ☆ ☆ ☆ ☆
AMBIENCE   ☆ ☆ ☆ ☆ ☆
AMENITIES   ☆ ☆ ☆ ☆ ☆
SOUND PROOFING   ☆ ☆ ☆ ☆ ☆
QUALITY OF THE FLUSH   ☆ ☆ ☆ ☆ ☆
TOILET PAPER   ☆ ☆ ☆ ☆ ☆

OVERALL EXPERIENCE:
☐ BEST SEAT IN THE HOUSE   ★ ★ ★ ★ ★
☐ WOULD POOP HERE AGAIN   ★ ★ ★ ★
☐ SHIT GOT REAL   ★ ★ ★
☐ SAME SHIT DIFFERENT HOUSE   ★ ★
☐ THINGS JUST DIDN'T COME OUT RIGHT   ★

THOUGHTS/MESSAGES: _____
_____
_____

Welcome! PLEASE SEAT YOURSELF AND ENJOY YOUR VISIT!

NAME: _____ DATE: _____ TIME: _____ DURATION OF VISIT: _____
                                                                              HRS   MIN   SEC

PURPOSE FOR VISIT: ⬜ #1 ⬜ #2 ⬜ OTHER: _____ SUCCESS? ⬜ YES ⬜ NO

FAVORITE EUPHEMISM FOR PERFORMING #1:   FAVORITE RESTROOM GRAFFITI OR YOUR ORIGNAL DOODLE:

FAVORITE EUPHEMISM FOR PERFORMING #2:

WHILE YOU WERE HERE, DID YOU:
- ☐ TEXT SOMEONE
- ☐ MAKE A PHONE CALL
- ☐ EMAIL
- ☐ CHECK SOCIAL MEDIA
- ☐ TAKE A SELFIE
- ☐ LOOK IN THE MEDICINE CABINET
- ☐ CHECK YOUR TEETH
- ☐ CHECK OUT YOUR BUTT
- ☐ CHECK YOUR FLY
- ☐ READ
- ☐ FIX YOUR HAIR
- ☐ TAKE SOME EXTRA "ME TIME"
- ☐ TALK TO YOURSELF
- ☐ CONDUCT BUSINESS OTHER THAN YOUR "BUSINESS." CARE TO SHARE?
  _____

FAVORITE NAME FOR THIS ROOM:
- ☐ BATHROOM
- ☐ TOILET
- ☐ POWDER ROOM
- ☐ LAVATORY
- ☐ SHITTER
- ☐ LOO
- ☐ LITTLE GIRLS ROOM
- ☐ LITTLE BOYS ROOM
- ☐ COMFORT STATION
- ☐ OTHER: _____
- ☐ JOHN
- ☐ CAN
- ☐ HEAD
- ☐ POTTY
- ☐ CRAPPER
- ☐ WC

_____

THOUGHTS/MESSAGES: _____
_____
_____

RATINGS: 1 2 3 4 5
CLEANLINESS   ☆ ☆ ☆ ☆ ☆
AMBIENCE   ☆ ☆ ☆ ☆ ☆
AMENITIES   ☆ ☆ ☆ ☆ ☆
SOUND PROOFING   ☆ ☆ ☆ ☆ ☆
QUALITY OF THE FLUSH   ☆ ☆ ☆ ☆ ☆
TOILET PAPER   ☆ ☆ ☆ ☆ ☆

OVERALL EXPERIENCE:
- ☐ BEST SEAT IN THE HOUSE   ★ ★ ★ ★ ★
- ☐ WOULD POOP HERE AGAIN   ★ ★ ★ ★
- ☐ SHIT GOT REAL   ★ ★ ★
- ☐ SAME SHIT DIFFERENT HOUSE   ★ ★
- ☐ THINGS JUST DIDN'T COME OUT RIGHT   ★

Welcome! PLEASE SEAT YOURSELF AND ENJOY YOUR VISIT!

NAME: _____ DATE: _____ TIME: _____ DURATION OF VISIT: _____
                                                                          HRS   MIN   SEC

PURPOSE FOR VISIT: 🧻 #1 🧻 #2 🧻 OTHER: _____ SUCCESS? 🧻 YES 🧻 NO

FAVORITE EUPHEMISM FOR PERFORMING #1: | FAVORITE RESTROOM GRAFFITI OR YOUR ORIGNAL DOODLE:

FAVORITE EUPHEMISM FOR PERFORMING #2:

WHILE YOU WERE HERE, DID YOU:
- ☐ TEXT SOMEONE
- ☐ MAKE A PHONE CALL
- ☐ EMAIL
- ☐ CHECK SOCIAL MEDIA
- ☐ TAKE A SELFIE
- ☐ LOOK IN THE MEDICINE CABINET
- ☐ CHECK YOUR TEETH
- ☐ CHECK OUT YOUR BUTT
- ☐ CHECK YOUR FLY
- ☐ READ
- ☐ FIX YOUR HAIR
- ☐ TAKE SOME EXTRA "ME TIME"
- ☐ TALK TO YOURSELF
- ☐ CONDUCT BUSINESS OTHER THAN YOUR "BUSINESS." CARE TO SHARE?
_____

FAVORITE NAME FOR THIS ROOM:
- ☐ BATHROOM
- ☐ TOILET
- ☐ POWDER ROOM
- ☐ LAVATORY
- ☐ SHITTER
- ☐ LOO
- ☐ LITTLE GIRLS ROOM
- ☐ LITTLE BOYS ROOM
- ☐ COMFORT STATION
- ☐ OTHER: _____

- ☐ JOHN
- ☐ CAN
- ☐ HEAD
- ☐ POTTY
- ☐ CRAPPER
- ☐ WC

_____

THOUGHTS/MESSAGES: _____
_____

RATINGS:

	1	2	3	4	5
CLEANLINESS	☆	☆	☆	☆	☆
AMBIENCE	☆	☆	☆	☆	☆
AMENITIES	☆	☆	☆	☆	☆
SOUND PROOFING	☆	☆	☆	☆	☆
QUALITY OF THE FLUSH	☆	☆	☆	☆	☆
TOILET PAPER	☆	☆	☆	☆	☆

OVERALL EXPERIENCE:
- ☐ BEST SEAT IN THE HOUSE ★★★★★
- ☐ WOULD POOP HERE AGAIN ★★★★
- ☐ SHIT GOT REAL ★★★
- ☐ SAME SHIT DIFFERENT HOUSE ★★
- ☐ THINGS JUST DIDN'T COME OUT RIGHT ★

Welcome! PLEASE SEAT YOURSELF AND ENJOY YOUR VISIT!

NAME: _____ DATE: _____ TIME: _____ DURATION OF VISIT: _____
HRS MIN SEC

PURPOSE FOR VISIT: ☐ #1 ☐ #2 ☐ OTHER: _____ SUCCESS? ☐ YES ☐ NO

FAVORITE EUPHEMISM FOR PERFORMING #1: | FAVORITE RESTROOM GRAFFITI OR YOUR ORIGNAL DOODLE:

FAVORITE EUPHEMISM FOR PERFORMING #2:

WHILE YOU WERE HERE, DID YOU:
- ☐ TEXT SOMEONE
- ☐ MAKE A PHONE CALL
- ☐ EMAIL
- ☐ CHECK SOCIAL MEDIA
- ☐ TAKE A SELFIE
- ☐ LOOK IN THE MEDICINE CABINET
- ☐ CHECK YOUR TEETH
- ☐ CHECK OUT YOUR BUTT
- ☐ CHECK YOUR FLY
- ☐ READ
- ☐ FIX YOUR HAIR
- ☐ TAKE SOME EXTRA "ME TIME"
- ☐ TALK TO YOURSELF
- ☐ CONDUCT BUSINESS OTHER THAN YOUR "BUSINESS." CARE TO SHARE?
_____

FAVORITE NAME FOR THIS ROOM:
- ☐ BATHROOM
- ☐ TOILET
- ☐ POWDER ROOM
- ☐ LAVATORY
- ☐ SHITTER
- ☐ LOO
- ☐ LITTLE GIRLS ROOM
- ☐ LITTLE BOYS ROOM
- ☐ COMFORT STATION
- ☐ OTHER: _____
- ☐ JOHN
- ☐ CAN
- ☐ HEAD
- ☐ POTTY
- ☐ CRAPPER
- ☐ WC

_____

THOUGHTS/MESSAGES: _____
_____
_____

RATINGS: 1 2 3 4 5
CLEANLINESS   ☆ ☆ ☆ ☆ ☆
AMBIENCE   ☆ ☆ ☆ ☆ ☆
AMENITIES   ☆ ☆ ☆ ☆ ☆
SOUND PROOFING   ☆ ☆ ☆ ☆ ☆
QUALITY OF THE FLUSH ☆ ☆ ☆ ☆ ☆
TOILET PAPER   ☆ ☆ ☆ ☆ ☆

OVERALL EXPERIENCE:
- ☐ BEST SEAT IN THE HOUSE ★ ★ ★ ★ ★
- ☐ WOULD POOP HERE AGAIN ★ ★ ★ ★
- ☐ SHIT GOT REAL ★ ★ ★
- ☐ SAME SHIT DIFFERENT HOUSE ★ ★
- ☐ THINGS JUST DIDN'T COME OUT RIGHT ★

Welcome! PLEASE SEAT YOURSELF AND ENJOY YOUR VISIT!

NAME: _____ DATE: _____ TIME: _____ DURATION OF VISIT: _____
HRS   MIN   SEC

PURPOSE FOR VISIT: ☐ #1 ☐ #2 ☐ OTHER: _____   SUCCESS? ☐ YES ☐ NO

FAVORITE EUPHEMISM FOR PERFORMING #1:

FAVORITE RESTROOM GRAFFITI OR YOUR ORIGNAL DOODLE:

FAVORITE EUPHEMISM FOR PERFORMING #2:

WHILE YOU WERE HERE, DID YOU:
☐ TEXT SOMEONE
☐ MAKE A PHONE CALL
☐ EMAIL
☐ CHECK SOCIAL MEDIA
☐ TAKE A SELFIE
☐ LOOK IN THE MEDICINE CABINET
☐ CHECK YOUR TEETH
☐ CHECK OUT YOUR BUTT
☐ CHECK YOUR FLY
☐ READ
☐ FIX YOUR HAIR
☐ TAKE SOME EXTRA "ME TIME"
☐ TALK TO YOURSELF
☐ CONDUCT BUSINESS OTHER THAN YOUR "BUSINESS." CARE TO SHARE?
_____

FAVORITE NAME FOR THIS ROOM:
☐ BATHROOM   ☐ JOHN
☐ TOILET   ☐ CAN
☐ POWDER ROOM   ☐ HEAD
☐ LAVATORY   ☐ POTTY
☐ SHITTER   ☐ CRAPPER
☐ LOO   ☐ WC
☐ LITTLE GIRLS ROOM
☐ LITTLE BOYS ROOM
☐ COMFORT STATION
☐ OTHER: _____
_____

THOUGHTS/MESSAGES: _____
_____
_____

RATINGS:
	1 2 3 4 5
CLEANLINESS	☆ ☆ ☆ ☆ ☆
AMBIENCE	☆ ☆ ☆ ☆ ☆
AMENITIES	☆ ☆ ☆ ☆ ☆
SOUND PROOFING	☆ ☆ ☆ ☆ ☆
QUALITY OF THE FLUSH	☆ ☆ ☆ ☆ ☆
TOILET PAPER	☆ ☆ ☆ ☆ ☆

OVERALL EXPERIENCE:
☐ BEST SEAT IN THE HOUSE ★ ★ ★ ★ ★
☐ WOULD POOP HERE AGAIN ★ ★ ★ ★
☐ SHIT GOT REAL ★ ★ ★
☐ SAME SHIT DIFFERENT HOUSE ★ ★
☐ THINGS JUST DIDN'T COME OUT RIGHT ★

Welcome! PLEASE SEAT YOURSELF AND ENJOY YOUR VISIT!

NAME: _____ DATE: _____ TIME: _____ DURATION OF VISIT: _____
HRS   MIN   SEC

PURPOSE FOR VISIT: ☐ #1 ☐ #2 ☐ OTHER: _____ SUCCESS? ☐ YES ☐ NO

FAVORITE EUPHEMISM FOR PERFORMING #1:

FAVORITE EUPHEMISM FOR PERFORMING #2:

FAVORITE RESTROOM GRAFFITI OR YOUR ORIGNAL DOODLE:

WHILE YOU WERE HERE, DID YOU:
☐ TEXT SOMEONE
☐ MAKE A PHONE CALL
☐ EMAIL
☐ CHECK SOCIAL MEDIA
☐ TAKE A SELFIE
☐ LOOK IN THE MEDICINE CABINET
☐ CHECK YOUR TEETH
☐ CHECK OUT YOUR BUTT
☐ CHECK YOUR FLY
☐ READ
☐ FIX YOUR HAIR
☐ TAKE SOME EXTRA "ME TIME"
☐ TALK TO YOURSELF
☐ CONDUCT BUSINESS OTHER THAN YOUR "BUSINESS." CARE TO SHARE?
_____

FAVORITE NAME FOR THIS ROOM:
☐ BATHROOM
☐ TOILET
☐ POWDER ROOM
☐ LAVATORY
☐ SHITTER
☐ LOO
☐ LITTLE GIRLS ROOM
☐ LITTLE BOYS ROOM
☐ COMFORT STATION
☐ OTHER: _____
☐ JOHN
☐ CAN
☐ HEAD
☐ POTTY
☐ CRAPPER
☐ WC

RATINGS:
	1	2	3	4	5
CLEANLINESS	☆	☆	☆	☆	☆
AMBIENCE	☆	☆	☆	☆	☆
AMENITIES	☆	☆	☆	☆	☆
SOUND PROOFING	☆	☆	☆	☆	☆
QUALITY OF THE FLUSH	☆	☆	☆	☆	☆
TOILET PAPER	☆	☆	☆	☆	☆

OVERALL EXPERIENCE:
☐ BEST SEAT IN THE HOUSE ★ ★ ★ ★ ★
☐ WOULD POOP HERE AGAIN ★ ★ ★ ★
☐ SHIT GOT REAL ★ ★ ★
☐ SAME SHIT DIFFERENT HOUSE ★ ★
☐ THINGS JUST DIDN'T COME OUT RIGHT ★

THOUGHTS/MESSAGES: _____
_____
_____

Welcome! PLEASE SEAT YOURSELF AND ENJOY YOUR VISIT!

NAME: _____ DATE: _____ TIME: _____ DURATION OF VISIT: _____
HRS   MIN   SEC

PURPOSE FOR VISIT: ☐ #1 ☐ #2 ☐ OTHER: _____ SUCCESS? ☐ YES ☐ NO

FAVORITE EUPHEMISM FOR PERFORMING #1:

FAVORITE RESTROOM GRAFFITI OR YOUR ORIGNAL DOODLE:

FAVORITE EUPHEMISM FOR PERFORMING #2:

WHILE YOU WERE HERE, DID YOU:
☐ TEXT SOMEONE
☐ MAKE A PHONE CALL
☐ EMAIL
☐ CHECK SOCIAL MEDIA
☐ TAKE A SELFIE
☐ LOOK IN THE MEDICINE CABINET
☐ CHECK YOUR TEETH
☐ CHECK OUT YOUR BUTT
☐ CHECK YOUR FLY
☐ READ
☐ FIX YOUR HAIR
☐ TAKE SOME EXTRA "ME TIME"
☐ TALK TO YOURSELF
☐ CONDUCT BUSINESS OTHER THAN
YOUR "BUSINESS." CARE TO SHARE?

_____

FAVORITE NAME FOR THIS ROOM:
☐ BATHROOM   ☐ JOHN
☐ TOILET   ☐ CAN
☐ POWDER ROOM   ☐ HEAD
☐ LAVATORY   ☐ POTTY
☐ SHITTER   ☐ CRAPPER
☐ LOO   ☐ WC
☐ LITTLE GIRLS ROOM
☐ LITTLE BOYS ROOM
☐ COMFORT STATION
☐ OTHER: _____

_____

THOUGHTS/MESSAGES: _____
_____
_____

RATINGS: 1 2 3 4 5
CLEANLINESS   ☆ ☆ ☆ ☆ ☆
AMBIENCE   ☆ ☆ ☆ ☆ ☆
AMENITIES   ☆ ☆ ☆ ☆ ☆
SOUND PROOFING   ☆ ☆ ☆ ☆ ☆
QUALITY OF THE FLUSH ☆ ☆ ☆ ☆ ☆
TOILET PAPER   ☆ ☆ ☆ ☆ ☆

OVERALL EXPERIENCE:
☐ BEST SEAT IN THE HOUSE   ★ ★ ★ ★ ★
☐ WOULD POOP HERE AGAIN   ★ ★ ★ ★
☐ SHIT GOT REAL   ★ ★ ★
☐ SAME SHIT DIFFERENT HOUSE   ★ ★
☐ THINGS JUST DIDN'T COME OUT RIGHT ★

Welcome! PLEASE SEAT YOURSELF AND ENJOY YOUR VISIT!

NAME: _____ DATE: _____ TIME: _____ DURATION OF VISIT: _____
HRS   MIN   SEC

PURPOSE FOR VISIT: 🧻 #1 🧻 #2 🧻 OTHER: _____ SUCCESS? 🧻 YES 🧻 NO

FAVORITE EUPHEMISM FOR PERFORMING #1:

FAVORITE RESTROOM GRAFFITI OR YOUR ORIGNAL DOODLE:

FAVORITE EUPHEMISM FOR PERFORMING #2:

WHILE YOU WERE HERE, DID YOU:
- ☐ TEXT SOMEONE
- ☐ MAKE A PHONE CALL
- ☐ EMAIL
- ☐ CHECK SOCIAL MEDIA
- ☐ TAKE A SELFIE
- ☐ LOOK IN THE MEDICINE CABINET
- ☐ CHECK YOUR TEETH
- ☐ CHECK OUT YOUR BUTT
- ☐ CHECK YOUR FLY
- ☐ READ
- ☐ FIX YOUR HAIR
- ☐ TAKE SOME EXTRA "ME TIME"
- ☐ TALK TO YOURSELF
- ☐ CONDUCT BUSINESS OTHER THAN YOUR "BUSINESS." CARE TO SHARE?
_____

FAVORITE NAME FOR THIS ROOM:
- ☐ BATHROOM
- ☐ TOILET
- ☐ POWDER ROOM
- ☐ LAVATORY
- ☐ SHITTER
- ☐ LOO
- ☐ LITTLE GIRLS ROOM
- ☐ LITTLE BOYS ROOM
- ☐ COMFORT STATION
- ☐ OTHER: _____

- ☐ JOHN
- ☐ CAN
- ☐ HEAD
- ☐ POTTY
- ☐ CRAPPER
- ☐ WC

_____

THOUGHTS/MESSAGES: _____
_____
_____

RATINGS:
	1	2	3	4	5
CLEANLINESS	☆	☆	☆	☆	☆
AMBIENCE	☆	☆	☆	☆	☆
AMENITIES	☆	☆	☆	☆	☆
SOUND PROOFING	☆	☆	☆	☆	☆
QUALITY OF THE FLUSH	☆	☆	☆	☆	☆
TOILET PAPER	☆	☆	☆	☆	☆

OVERALL EXPERIENCE:
- ☐ BEST SEAT IN THE HOUSE ★ ★ ★ ★ ★
- ☐ WOULD POOP HERE AGAIN ★ ★ ★ ★
- ☐ SHIT GOT REAL ★ ★ ★
- ☐ SAME SHIT DIFFERENT HOUSE ★ ★
- ☐ THINGS JUST DIDN'T COME OUT RIGHT ★

Welcome! PLEASE SEAT YOURSELF AND ENJOY YOUR VISIT!

NAME: _____ DATE: _____ TIME: _____ DURATION OF VISIT: _____

HRS   MIN   SEC

PURPOSE FOR VISIT: [ ] #1 [ ] #2 [ ] OTHER: _____ SUCCESS? [ ] YES [ ] NO

FAVORITE EUPHEMISM FOR PERFORMING #1:

FAVORITE RESTROOM GRAFFITI OR YOUR ORIGNAL DOODLE:

FAVORITE EUPHEMISM FOR PERFORMING #2:

WHILE YOU WERE HERE, DID YOU:
- [ ] TEXT SOMEONE
- [ ] MAKE A PHONE CALL
- [ ] EMAIL
- [ ] CHECK SOCIAL MEDIA
- [ ] TAKE A SELFIE
- [ ] LOOK IN THE MEDICINE CABINET
- [ ] CHECK YOUR TEETH
- [ ] CHECK OUT YOUR BUTT
- [ ] CHECK YOUR FLY
- [ ] READ
- [ ] FIX YOUR HAIR
- [ ] TAKE SOME EXTRA "ME TIME"
- [ ] TALK TO YOURSELF
- [ ] CONDUCT BUSINESS OTHER THAN YOUR "BUSINESS." CARE TO SHARE?

FAVORITE NAME FOR THIS ROOM:
- [ ] BATHROOM
- [ ] TOILET
- [ ] POWDER ROOM
- [ ] LAVATORY
- [ ] SHITTER
- [ ] LOO
- [ ] LITTLE GIRLS ROOM
- [ ] LITTLE BOYS ROOM
- [ ] COMFORT STATION
- [ ] OTHER: _____
- [ ] JOHN
- [ ] CAN
- [ ] HEAD
- [ ] POTTY
- [ ] CRAPPER
- [ ] WC

_____

THOUGHTS/MESSAGES: _____

RATINGS:

	1	2	3	4	5
CLEANLINESS	☆	☆	☆	☆	☆
AMBIENCE	☆	☆	☆	☆	☆
AMENITIES	☆	☆	☆	☆	☆
SOUND PROOFING	☆	☆	☆	☆	☆
QUALITY OF THE FLUSH	☆	☆	☆	☆	☆
TOILET PAPER	☆	☆	☆	☆	☆

OVERALL EXPERIENCE:
- [ ] BEST SEAT IN THE HOUSE ★ ★ ★ ★ ★
- [ ] WOULD POOP HERE AGAIN ★ ★ ★ ★
- [ ] SHIT GOT REAL ★ ★ ★
- [ ] SAME SHIT DIFFERENT HOUSE ★ ★
- [ ] THINGS JUST DIDN'T COME OUT RIGHT ★

NAME: _____ DATE: _____ TIME: _____ DURATION OF VISIT: _____
HRS   MIN   SEC

PURPOSE FOR VISIT: ☐ #1 ☐ #2 ☐ OTHER: _____ SUCCESS? ☐ YES ☐ NO

FAVORITE EUPHEMISM FOR PERFORMING #1:

FAVORITE RESTROOM GRAFFITI OR YOUR ORIGNAL DOODLE:

FAVORITE EUPHEMISM FOR PERFORMING #2:

WHILE YOU WERE HERE, DID YOU:
☐ TEXT SOMEONE
☐ MAKE A PHONE CALL
☐ EMAIL
☐ CHECK SOCIAL MEDIA
☐ TAKE A SELFIE
☐ LOOK IN THE MEDICINE CABINET
☐ CHECK YOUR TEETH
☐ CHECK OUT YOUR BUTT
☐ CHECK YOUR FLY
☐ READ
☐ FIX YOUR HAIR
☐ TAKE SOME EXTRA "ME TIME"
☐ TALK TO YOURSELF
☐ CONDUCT BUSINESS OTHER THAN YOUR "BUSINESS." CARE TO SHARE?
_____

FAVORITE NAME FOR THIS ROOM:
☐ BATHROOM   ☐ JOHN
☐ TOILET   ☐ CAN
☐ POWDER ROOM   ☐ HEAD
☐ LAVATORY   ☐ POTTY
☐ SHITTER   ☐ CRAPPER
☐ LOO   ☐ WC
☐ LITTLE GIRLS ROOM
☐ LITTLE BOYS ROOM
☐ COMFORT STATION
☐ OTHER: _____
_____

RATINGS: 1 2 3 4 5
CLEANLINESS   ☆ ☆ ☆ ☆ ☆
AMBIENCE   ☆ ☆ ☆ ☆ ☆
AMENITIES   ☆ ☆ ☆ ☆ ☆
SOUND PROOFING   ☆ ☆ ☆ ☆ ☆
QUALITY OF THE FLUSH ☆ ☆ ☆ ☆ ☆
TOILET PAPER   ☆ ☆ ☆ ☆ ☆

OVERALL EXPERIENCE:
☐ BEST SEAT IN THE HOUSE ★ ★ ★ ★ ★
☐ WOULD POOP HERE AGAIN ★ ★ ★ ★
☐ SHIT GOT REAL ★ ★ ★
☐ SAME SHIT DIFFERENT HOUSE ★ ★
☐ THINGS JUST DIDN'T COME OUT RIGHT ★

THOUGHTS/MESSAGES: _____
_____
_____

Welcome! PLEASE SEAT YOURSELF AND ENJOY YOUR VISIT!

NAME: _____ DATE: _____ TIME: _____ DURATION OF VISIT: _____

HRS   MIN   SEC

PURPOSE FOR VISIT: 🧻 #1 🧻 #2 🧻 OTHER: _____ SUCCESS? 🧻 YES 🧻 NO

FAVORITE EUPHEMISM FOR PERFORMING #1:

FAVORITE RESTROOM GRAFFITI OR YOUR ORIGNAL DOODLE:

FAVORITE EUPHEMISM FOR PERFORMING #2:

WHILE YOU WERE HERE, DID YOU:
☐ TEXT SOMEONE
☐ MAKE A PHONE CALL
☐ EMAIL
☐ CHECK SOCIAL MEDIA
☐ TAKE A SELFIE
☐ LOOK IN THE MEDICINE CABINET
☐ CHECK YOUR TEETH
☐ CHECK OUT YOUR BUTT
☐ CHECK YOUR FLY
☐ READ
☐ FIX YOUR HAIR
☐ TAKE SOME EXTRA "ME TIME"
☐ TALK TO YOURSELF
☐ CONDUCT BUSINESS OTHER THAN YOUR "BUSINESS." CARE TO SHARE?

FAVORITE NAME FOR THIS ROOM:
☐ BATHROOM   ☐ JOHN
☐ TOILET   ☐ CAN
☐ POWDER ROOM   ☐ HEAD
☐ LAVATORY   ☐ POTTY
☐ SHITTER   ☐ CRAPPER
☐ LOO   ☐ WC
☐ LITTLE GIRLS ROOM
☐ LITTLE BOYS ROOM
☐ COMFORT STATION
☐ OTHER: _____
_____

THOUGHTS/MESSAGES: _____
_____
_____

RATINGS: 1 2 3 4 5
CLEANLINESS   ☆ ☆ ☆ ☆ ☆
AMBIENCE   ☆ ☆ ☆ ☆ ☆
AMENITIES   ☆ ☆ ☆ ☆ ☆
SOUND PROOFING   ☆ ☆ ☆ ☆ ☆
QUALITY OF THE FLUSH   ☆ ☆ ☆ ☆ ☆
TOILET PAPER   ☆ ☆ ☆ ☆ ☆

OVERALL EXPERIENCE:
☐ BEST SEAT IN THE HOUSE   ★ ★ ★ ★ ★
☐ WOULD POOP HERE AGAIN   ★ ★ ★ ★
☐ SHIT GOT REAL   ★ ★ ★
☐ SAME SHIT DIFFERENT HOUSE   ★ ★
☐ THINGS JUST DIDN'T COME OUT RIGHT ★

Welcome! PLEASE SEAT YOURSELF AND ENJOY YOUR VISIT!

NAME: _____ DATE: _____ TIME: _____ DURATION OF VISIT: _____
                                                                    HRS   MIN   SEC

PURPOSE FOR VISIT: 🧻 #1 🧻 #2 🧻 OTHER: _____ SUCCESS? 🧻 YES 🧻 NO

FAVORITE EUPHEMISM FOR PERFORMING #1:

FAVORITE RESTROOM GRAFFITI OR YOUR ORIGNAL DOODLE:

FAVORITE EUPHEMISM FOR PERFORMING #2:

WHILE YOU WERE HERE, DID YOU:
- ☐ TEXT SOMEONE
- ☐ MAKE A PHONE CALL
- ☐ EMAIL
- ☐ CHECK SOCIAL MEDIA
- ☐ TAKE A SELFIE
- ☐ LOOK IN THE MEDICINE CABINET
- ☐ CHECK YOUR TEETH
- ☐ CHECK OUT YOUR BUTT
- ☐ CHECK YOUR FLY
- ☐ READ
- ☐ FIX YOUR HAIR
- ☐ TAKE SOME EXTRA "ME TIME"
- ☐ TALK TO YOURSELF
- ☐ CONDUCT BUSINESS OTHER THAN YOUR "BUSINESS." CARE TO SHARE?
_____

FAVORITE NAME FOR THIS ROOM:
- ☐ BATHROOM
- ☐ TOILET
- ☐ POWDER ROOM
- ☐ LAVATORY
- ☐ SHITTER
- ☐ LOO
- ☐ LITTLE GIRLS ROOM
- ☐ LITTLE BOYS ROOM
- ☐ COMFORT STATION
- ☐ OTHER: _____
- ☐ JOHN
- ☐ CAN
- ☐ HEAD
- ☐ POTTY
- ☐ CRAPPER
- ☐ WC

_____

THOUGHTS/MESSAGES: _____
_____
_____

RATINGS:

	1	2	3	4	5
CLEANLINESS	☆	☆	☆	☆	☆
AMBIENCE	☆	☆	☆	☆	☆
AMENITIES	☆	☆	☆	☆	☆
SOUND PROOFING	☆	☆	☆	☆	☆
QUALITY OF THE FLUSH	☆	☆	☆	☆	☆
TOILET PAPER	☆	☆	☆	☆	☆

OVERALL EXPERIENCE:
- ☐ BEST SEAT IN THE HOUSE ★★★★★
- ☐ WOULD POOP HERE AGAIN ★★★★
- ☐ SHIT GOT REAL ★★★
- ☐ SAME SHIT DIFFERENT HOUSE ★★
- ☐ THINGS JUST DIDN'T COME OUT RIGHT ★

Welcome! PLEASE SEAT YOURSELF AND ENJOY YOUR VISIT!

NAME: _____ DATE: _____ TIME: _____ DURATION OF VISIT: _____
HRS   MIN   SEC

PURPOSE FOR VISIT: ☐ #1 ☐ #2 ☐ OTHER: _____ SUCCESS? ☐ YES ☐ NO

FAVORITE EUPHEMISM FOR PERFORMING #1:

FAVORITE RESTROOM GRAFFITI OR YOUR ORIGNAL DOODLE:

FAVORITE EUPHEMISM FOR PERFORMING #2:

WHILE YOU WERE HERE, DID YOU:
☐ TEXT SOMEONE
☐ MAKE A PHONE CALL
☐ EMAIL
☐ CHECK SOCIAL MEDIA
☐ TAKE A SELFIE
☐ LOOK IN THE MEDICINE CABINET
☐ CHECK YOUR TEETH
☐ CHECK OUT YOUR BUTT
☐ CHECK YOUR FLY
☐ READ
☐ FIX YOUR HAIR
☐ TAKE SOME EXTRA "ME TIME"
☐ TALK TO YOURSELF
☐ CONDUCT BUSINESS OTHER THAN YOUR "BUSINESS." CARE TO SHARE?
_____

FAVORITE NAME FOR THIS ROOM:
☐ BATHROOM   ☐ JOHN
☐ TOILET   ☐ CAN
☐ POWDER ROOM   ☐ HEAD
☐ LAVATORY   ☐ POTTY
☐ SHITTER   ☐ CRAPPER
☐ LOO   ☐ WC
☐ LITTLE GIRLS ROOM
☐ LITTLE BOYS ROOM
☐ COMFORT STATION
☐ OTHER: _____
_____

THOUGHTS/MESSAGES: _____
_____
_____

RATINGS: 1 2 3 4 5
CLEANLINESS   ☆ ☆ ☆ ☆ ☆
AMBIENCE   ☆ ☆ ☆ ☆ ☆
AMENITIES   ☆ ☆ ☆ ☆ ☆
SOUND PROOFING   ☆ ☆ ☆ ☆ ☆
QUALITY OF THE FLUSH ☆ ☆ ☆ ☆ ☆
TOILET PAPER   ☆ ☆ ☆ ☆ ☆

OVERALL EXPERIENCE:
☐ BEST SEAT IN THE HOUSE   ★ ★ ★ ★ ★
☐ WOULD POOP HERE AGAIN   ★ ★ ★ ★
☐ SHIT GOT REAL   ★ ★ ★
☐ SAME SHIT DIFFERENT HOUSE   ★ ★
☐ THINGS JUST DIDN'T COME OUT RIGHT ★

Welcome! PLEASE SEAT YOURSELF AND ENJOY YOUR VISIT!

NAME: _____ DATE: _____ TIME: _____ DURATION OF VISIT: _____
HRS   MIN   SEC

PURPOSE FOR VISIT: ▢ #1 ▢ #2 ▢ OTHER: _____ SUCCESS? ▢ YES ▢ NO

FAVORITE EUPHEMISM FOR PERFORMING #1:

FAVORITE RESTROOM GRAFFITI OR YOUR ORIGNAL DOODLE:

FAVORITE EUPHEMISM FOR PERFORMING #2:

WHILE YOU WERE HERE, DID YOU:
- ☐ TEXT SOMEONE
- ☐ MAKE A PHONE CALL
- ☐ EMAIL
- ☐ CHECK SOCIAL MEDIA
- ☐ TAKE A SELFIE
- ☐ LOOK IN THE MEDICINE CABINET
- ☐ CHECK YOUR TEETH
- ☐ CHECK OUT YOUR BUTT
- ☐ CHECK YOUR FLY
- ☐ READ
- ☐ FIX YOUR HAIR
- ☐ TAKE SOME EXTRA "ME TIME"
- ☐ TALK TO YOURSELF
- ☐ CONDUCT BUSINESS OTHER THAN YOUR "BUSINESS." CARE TO SHARE?
_____

FAVORITE NAME FOR THIS ROOM:
- ☐ BATHROOM
- ☐ TOILET
- ☐ POWDER ROOM
- ☐ LAVATORY
- ☐ SHITTER
- ☐ LOO
- ☐ LITTLE GIRLS ROOM
- ☐ LITTLE BOYS ROOM
- ☐ COMFORT STATION
- ☐ OTHER: _____
- ☐ JOHN
- ☐ CAN
- ☐ HEAD
- ☐ POTTY
- ☐ CRAPPER
- ☐ WC

_____

RATINGS:
	1 2 3 4 5
CLEANLINESS	☆ ☆ ☆ ☆ ☆
AMBIENCE	☆ ☆ ☆ ☆ ☆
AMENITIES	☆ ☆ ☆ ☆ ☆
SOUND PROOFING	☆ ☆ ☆ ☆ ☆
QUALITY OF THE FLUSH	☆ ☆ ☆ ☆ ☆
TOILET PAPER	☆ ☆ ☆ ☆ ☆

OVERALL EXPERIENCE:
- ☐ BEST SEAT IN THE HOUSE ★ ★ ★ ★ ★
- ☐ WOULD POOP HERE AGAIN ★ ★ ★ ★
- ☐ SHIT GOT REAL ★ ★ ★
- ☐ SAME SHIT DIFFERENT HOUSE ★ ★
- ☐ THINGS JUST DIDN'T COME OUT RIGHT ★

THOUGHTS/MESSAGES: _____
_____
_____

Welcome! PLEASE SEAT YOURSELF AND ENJOY YOUR VISIT!

NAME: _____ DATE: _____ TIME: _____ DURATION OF VISIT: _____
HRS   MIN   SEC

PURPOSE FOR VISIT: ☐ #1 ☐ #2 ☐ OTHER: _____ SUCCESS? ☐ YES ☐ NO

FAVORITE EUPHEMISM FOR PERFORMING #1:

FAVORITE RESTROOM GRAFFITI OR YOUR ORIGNAL DOODLE:

FAVORITE EUPHEMISM FOR PERFORMING #2:

WHILE YOU WERE HERE, DID YOU:
☐ TEXT SOMEONE
☐ MAKE A PHONE CALL
☐ EMAIL
☐ CHECK SOCIAL MEDIA
☐ TAKE A SELFIE
☐ LOOK IN THE MEDICINE CABINET
☐ CHECK YOUR TEETH
☐ CHECK OUT YOUR BUTT
☐ CHECK YOUR FLY
☐ READ
☐ FIX YOUR HAIR
☐ TAKE SOME EXTRA "ME TIME"
☐ TALK TO YOURSELF
☐ CONDUCT BUSINESS OTHER THAN YOUR "BUSINESS." CARE TO SHARE?
_____

FAVORITE NAME FOR THIS ROOM:
☐ BATHROOM
☐ TOILET
☐ POWDER ROOM
☐ LAVATORY
☐ SHITTER
☐ LOO
☐ LITTLE GIRLS ROOM
☐ LITTLE BOYS ROOM
☐ COMFORT STATION
☐ OTHER: _____

☐ JOHN
☐ CAN
☐ HEAD
☐ POTTY
☐ CRAPPER
☐ WC

RATINGS: 1 2 3 4 5
CLEANLINESS   ☆ ☆ ☆ ☆ ☆
AMBIENCE   ☆ ☆ ☆ ☆ ☆
AMENITIES   ☆ ☆ ☆ ☆ ☆
SOUND PROOFING   ☆ ☆ ☆ ☆ ☆
QUALITY OF THE FLUSH   ☆ ☆ ☆ ☆ ☆
TOILET PAPER   ☆ ☆ ☆ ☆ ☆

OVERALL EXPERIENCE:
☐ BEST SEAT IN THE HOUSE   ★ ★ ★ ★ ★
☐ WOULD POOP HERE AGAIN   ★ ★ ★ ★
☐ SHIT GOT REAL   ★ ★ ★
☐ SAME SHIT DIFFERENT HOUSE   ★ ★
☐ THINGS JUST DIDN'T COME OUT RIGHT ★

THOUGHTS/MESSAGES: _____
_____
_____

Welcome! PLEASE SEAT YOURSELF AND ENJOY YOUR VISIT!

NAME: _____ DATE: _____ TIME: _____ DURATION OF VISIT: _____
HRS   MIN   SEC

PURPOSE FOR VISIT: 🧻 #1 🧻 #2 🧻 OTHER: _____ SUCCESS? 🧻 YES 🧻 NO

FAVORITE EUPHEMISM FOR PERFORMING #1:

FAVORITE RESTROOM GRAFFITI OR YOUR ORIGNAL DOODLE:

FAVORITE EUPHEMISM FOR PERFORMING #2:

WHILE YOU WERE HERE, DID YOU:
- ☐ TEXT SOMEONE
- ☐ MAKE A PHONE CALL
- ☐ EMAIL
- ☐ CHECK SOCIAL MEDIA
- ☐ TAKE A SELFIE
- ☐ LOOK IN THE MEDICINE CABINET
- ☐ CHECK YOUR TEETH
- ☐ CHECK OUT YOUR BUTT
- ☐ CHECK YOUR FLY
- ☐ READ
- ☐ FIX YOUR HAIR
- ☐ TAKE SOME EXTRA "ME TIME"
- ☐ TALK TO YOURSELF
- ☐ CONDUCT BUSINESS OTHER THAN YOUR "BUSINESS." CARE TO SHARE?
  _____

FAVORITE NAME FOR THIS ROOM:
- ☐ BATHROOM
- ☐ TOILET
- ☐ POWDER ROOM
- ☐ LAVATORY
- ☐ SHITTER
- ☐ LOO
- ☐ LITTLE GIRLS ROOM
- ☐ LITTLE BOYS ROOM
- ☐ COMFORT STATION
- ☐ OTHER: _____

- ☐ JOHN
- ☐ CAN
- ☐ HEAD
- ☐ POTTY
- ☐ CRAPPER
- ☐ WC

RATINGS:
	1	2	3	4	5
CLEANLINESS	☆	☆	☆	☆	☆
AMBIENCE	☆	☆	☆	☆	☆
AMENITIES	☆	☆	☆	☆	☆
SOUND PROOFING	☆	☆	☆	☆	☆
QUALITY OF THE FLUSH	☆	☆	☆	☆	☆
TOILET PAPER	☆	☆	☆	☆	☆

OVERALL EXPERIENCE:
- ☐ BEST SEAT IN THE HOUSE ★ ★ ★ ★ ★
- ☐ WOULD POOP HERE AGAIN ★ ★ ★ ★
- ☐ SHIT GOT REAL ★ ★ ★
- ☐ SAME SHIT DIFFERENT HOUSE ★ ★
- ☐ THINGS JUST DIDN'T COME OUT RIGHT ★

THOUGHTS/MESSAGES: _____

Welcome! PLEASE SEAT YOURSELF AND ENJOY YOUR VISIT!

NAME: _____ DATE: _____ TIME: _____ DURATION OF VISIT: _____

HRS   MIN   SEC

PURPOSE FOR VISIT: 🧻 #1 🧻 #2 🧻 OTHER: _____   SUCCESS? 🧻 YES 🧻 NO

FAVORITE EUPHEMISM FOR PERFORMING #1:

FAVORITE RESTROOM GRAFFITI OR YOUR ORIGNAL DOODLE:

FAVORITE EUPHEMISM FOR PERFORMING #2:

WHILE YOU WERE HERE, DID YOU:

- ☐ TEXT SOMEONE
- ☐ MAKE A PHONE CALL
- ☐ EMAIL
- ☐ CHECK SOCIAL MEDIA
- ☐ TAKE A SELFIE
- ☐ LOOK IN THE MEDICINE CABINET
- ☐ CHECK YOUR TEETH
- ☐ CHECK OUT YOUR BUTT
- ☐ CHECK YOUR FLY
- ☐ READ
- ☐ FIX YOUR HAIR
- ☐ TAKE SOME EXTRA "ME TIME"
- ☐ TALK TO YOURSELF
- ☐ CONDUCT BUSINESS OTHER THAN YOUR "BUSINESS." CARE TO SHARE?

FAVORITE NAME FOR THIS ROOM:

- ☐ BATHROOM
- ☐ TOILET
- ☐ POWDER ROOM
- ☐ LAVATORY
- ☐ SHITTER
- ☐ LOO
- ☐ LITTLE GIRLS ROOM
- ☐ LITTLE BOYS ROOM
- ☐ COMFORT STATION
- ☐ OTHER: _____

- ☐ JOHN
- ☐ CAN
- ☐ HEAD
- ☐ POTTY
- ☐ CRAPPER
- ☐ WC

_____

RATINGS:

	1	2	3	4	5
CLEANLINESS	☆	☆	☆	☆	☆
AMBIENCE	☆	☆	☆	☆	☆
AMENITIES	☆	☆	☆	☆	☆
SOUND PROOFING	☆	☆	☆	☆	☆
QUALITY OF THE FLUSH	☆	☆	☆	☆	☆
TOILET PAPER	☆	☆	☆	☆	☆

OVERALL EXPERIENCE:

- ☐ BEST SEAT IN THE HOUSE ★ ★ ★ ★ ★
- ☐ WOULD POOP HERE AGAIN ★ ★ ★ ★
- ☐ SHIT GOT REAL ★ ★ ★
- ☐ SAME SHIT DIFFERENT HOUSE ★ ★
- ☐ THINGS JUST DIDN'T COME OUT RIGHT ★

THOUGHTS/MESSAGES: _____

_____

_____

Welcome! PLEASE SEAT YOURSELF AND ENJOY YOUR VISIT!

NAME: _____ DATE: _____ TIME: _____ DURATION OF VISIT: _____
HRS   MIN   SEC

PURPOSE FOR VISIT: ☐ #1 ☐ #2 ☐ OTHER: _____   SUCCESS? ☐ YES ☐ NO

FAVORITE EUPHEMISM FOR PERFORMING #1:

FAVORITE EUPHEMISM FOR PERFORMING #2:

FAVORITE RESTROOM GRAFFITI OR YOUR ORIGNAL DOODLE:

WHILE YOU WERE HERE, DID YOU:
☐ TEXT SOMEONE
☐ MAKE A PHONE CALL
☐ EMAIL
☐ CHECK SOCIAL MEDIA
☐ TAKE A SELFIE
☐ LOOK IN THE MEDICINE CABINET
☐ CHECK YOUR TEETH
☐ CHECK OUT YOUR BUTT
☐ CHECK YOUR FLY
☐ READ
☐ FIX YOUR HAIR
☐ TAKE SOME EXTRA "ME TIME"
☐ TALK TO YOURSELF
☐ CONDUCT BUSINESS OTHER THAN YOUR "BUSINESS." CARE TO SHARE?
_____

FAVORITE NAME FOR THIS ROOM:
☐ BATHROOM   ☐ JOHN
☐ TOILET   ☐ CAN
☐ POWDER ROOM   ☐ HEAD
☐ LAVATORY   ☐ POTTY
☐ SHITTER   ☐ CRAPPER
☐ LOO   ☐ WC
☐ LITTLE GIRLS ROOM
☐ LITTLE BOYS ROOM
☐ COMFORT STATION
☐ OTHER: _____

_____

THOUGHTS/MESSAGES: _____
_____
_____

RATINGS: 1 2 3 4 5
CLEANLINESS   ☆ ☆ ☆ ☆ ☆
AMBIENCE   ☆ ☆ ☆ ☆ ☆
AMENITIES   ☆ ☆ ☆ ☆ ☆
SOUND PROOFING   ☆ ☆ ☆ ☆ ☆
QUALITY OF THE FLUSH ☆ ☆ ☆ ☆ ☆
TOILET PAPER   ☆ ☆ ☆ ☆ ☆

OVERALL EXPERIENCE:
☐ BEST SEAT IN THE HOUSE   ★ ★ ★ ★ ★
☐ WOULD POOP HERE AGAIN   ★ ★ ★ ★
☐ SHIT GOT REAL   ★ ★ ★
☐ SAME SHIT DIFFERENT HOUSE   ★ ★
☐ THINGS JUST DIDN'T COME OUT RIGHT   ★

Welcome! PLEASE SEAT YOURSELF AND ENJOY YOUR VISIT!

NAME: _____ DATE: _____ TIME: _____ DURATION OF VISIT: _____
HRS   MIN   SEC

PURPOSE FOR VISIT: ☐ #1 ☐ #2 ☐ OTHER: _____ SUCCESS? ☐ YES ☐ NO

FAVORITE EUPHEMISM FOR PERFORMING #1:

FAVORITE RESTROOM GRAFFITI OR YOUR ORIGNAL DOODLE:

FAVORITE EUPHEMISM FOR PERFORMING #2:

WHILE YOU WERE HERE, DID YOU:
☐ TEXT SOMEONE
☐ MAKE A PHONE CALL
☐ EMAIL
☐ CHECK SOCIAL MEDIA
☐ TAKE A SELFIE
☐ LOOK IN THE MEDICINE CABINET
☐ CHECK YOUR TEETH
☐ CHECK OUT YOUR BUTT
☐ CHECK YOUR FLY
☐ READ
☐ FIX YOUR HAIR
☐ TAKE SOME EXTRA "ME TIME"
☐ TALK TO YOURSELF
☐ CONDUCT BUSINESS OTHER THAN YOUR "BUSINESS." CARE TO SHARE?
_____

FAVORITE NAME FOR THIS ROOM:
☐ BATHROOM   ☐ JOHN
☐ TOILET   ☐ CAN
☐ POWDER ROOM   ☐ HEAD
☐ LAVATORY   ☐ POTTY
☐ SHITTER   ☐ CRAPPER
☐ LOO   ☐ WC
☐ LITTLE GIRLS ROOM
☐ LITTLE BOYS ROOM
☐ COMFORT STATION
☐ OTHER: _____
_____

RATINGS: 1 2 3 4 5
CLEANLINESS   ☆ ☆ ☆ ☆ ☆
AMBIENCE   ☆ ☆ ☆ ☆ ☆
AMENITIES   ☆ ☆ ☆ ☆ ☆
SOUND PROOFING   ☆ ☆ ☆ ☆ ☆
QUALITY OF THE FLUSH ☆ ☆ ☆ ☆ ☆
TOILET PAPER   ☆ ☆ ☆ ☆ ☆

OVERALL EXPERIENCE:
☐ BEST SEAT IN THE HOUSE   ★ ★ ★ ★ ★
☐ WOULD POOP HERE AGAIN   ★ ★ ★ ★
☐ SHIT GOT REAL   ★ ★ ★
☐ SAME SHIT DIFFERENT HOUSE   ★ ★
☐ THINGS JUST DIDN'T COME OUT RIGHT ★

THOUGHTS/MESSAGES: _____
_____

NAME: _____ DATE: _____ TIME: _____ DURATION OF VISIT: _____

HRS   MIN   SEC

PURPOSE FOR VISIT: 🧻 #1 🧻 #2 🧻 OTHER: _____ SUCCESS? 🧻 YES 🧻 NO

FAVORITE EUPHEMISM FOR PERFORMING #1: | FAVORITE RESTROOM GRAFFITI OR YOUR ORIGNAL DOODLE:

FAVORITE EUPHEMISM FOR PERFORMING #2:

WHILE YOU WERE HERE, DID YOU:
- ☐ TEXT SOMEONE
- ☐ MAKE A PHONE CALL
- ☐ EMAIL
- ☐ CHECK SOCIAL MEDIA
- ☐ TAKE A SELFIE
- ☐ LOOK IN THE MEDICINE CABINET
- ☐ CHECK YOUR TEETH
- ☐ CHECK OUT YOUR BUTT
- ☐ CHECK YOUR FLY
- ☐ READ
- ☐ FIX YOUR HAIR
- ☐ TAKE SOME EXTRA "ME TIME"
- ☐ TALK TO YOURSELF
- ☐ CONDUCT BUSINESS OTHER THAN YOUR "BUSINESS." CARE TO SHARE?
  _____

FAVORITE NAME FOR THIS ROOM:
- ☐ BATHROOM
- ☐ TOILET
- ☐ POWDER ROOM
- ☐ LAVATORY
- ☐ SHITTER
- ☐ LOO
- ☐ LITTLE GIRLS ROOM
- ☐ LITTLE BOYS ROOM
- ☐ COMFORT STATION
- ☐ OTHER: _____
- ☐ JOHN
- ☐ CAN
- ☐ HEAD
- ☐ POTTY
- ☐ CRAPPER
- ☐ WC

_____

RATINGS:	1	2	3	4	5
CLEANLINESS	☆	☆	☆	☆	☆
AMBIENCE	☆	☆	☆	☆	☆
AMENITIES	☆	☆	☆	☆	☆
SOUND PROOFING	☆	☆	☆	☆	☆
QUALITY OF THE FLUSH	☆	☆	☆	☆	☆
TOILET PAPER	☆	☆	☆	☆	☆

OVERALL EXPERIENCE:
- ☐ BEST SEAT IN THE HOUSE ★ ★ ★ ★ ★
- ☐ WOULD POOP HERE AGAIN ★ ★ ★ ★
- ☐ SHIT GOT REAL ★ ★ ★
- ☐ SAME SHIT DIFFERENT HOUSE ★ ★
- ☐ THINGS JUST DIDN'T COME OUT RIGHT ★

THOUGHTS/MESSAGES: _____
_____
_____

Welcome! PLEASE SEAT YOURSELF AND ENJOY YOUR VISIT!

NAME: _____ DATE: _____ TIME: _____ DURATION OF VISIT: _____

HRS   MIN   SEC

PURPOSE FOR VISIT: ▯ #1 ▯ #2 ▯ OTHER: _____   SUCCESS? ▯ YES ▯ NO

FAVORITE EUPHEMISM FOR PERFORMING #1:

FAVORITE RESTROOM GRAFFITI OR YOUR ORIGNAL DOODLE:

FAVORITE EUPHEMISM FOR PERFORMING #2:

WHILE YOU WERE HERE, DID YOU:
- ▢ TEXT SOMEONE
- ▢ MAKE A PHONE CALL
- ▢ EMAIL
- ▢ CHECK SOCIAL MEDIA
- ▢ TAKE A SELFIE
- ▢ LOOK IN THE MEDICINE CABINET
- ▢ CHECK YOUR TEETH
- ▢ CHECK OUT YOUR BUTT
- ▢ CHECK YOUR FLY
- ▢ READ
- ▢ FIX YOUR HAIR
- ▢ TAKE SOME EXTRA "ME TIME"
- ▢ TALK TO YOURSELF
- ▢ CONDUCT BUSINESS OTHER THAN YOUR "BUSINESS." CARE TO SHARE?
_____

FAVORITE NAME FOR THIS ROOM:
- ▢ BATHROOM
- ▢ TOILET
- ▢ POWDER ROOM
- ▢ LAVATORY
- ▢ SHITTER
- ▢ LOO
- ▢ LITTLE GIRLS ROOM
- ▢ LITTLE BOYS ROOM
- ▢ COMFORT STATION
- ▢ OTHER: _____
- ▢ JOHN
- ▢ CAN
- ▢ HEAD
- ▢ POTTY
- ▢ CRAPPER
- ▢ WC

_____

THOUGHTS/MESSAGES: _____

_____

_____

RATINGS: 1 2 3 4 5
CLEANLINESS	☆ ☆ ☆ ☆ ☆
AMBIENCE	☆ ☆ ☆ ☆ ☆
AMENITIES	☆ ☆ ☆ ☆ ☆
SOUND PROOFING	☆ ☆ ☆ ☆ ☆
QUALITY OF THE FLUSH	☆ ☆ ☆ ☆ ☆
TOILET PAPER	☆ ☆ ☆ ☆ ☆

OVERALL EXPERIENCE:
- ▢ BEST SEAT IN THE HOUSE ★ ★ ★ ★ ★
- ▢ WOULD POOP HERE AGAIN ★ ★ ★ ★
- ▢ SHIT GOT REAL ★ ★ ★
- ▢ SAME SHIT DIFFERENT HOUSE ★ ★
- ▢ THINGS JUST DIDN'T COME OUT RIGHT ★

Welcome! PLEASE SEAT YOURSELF AND ENJOY YOUR VISIT!

NAME: _____ DATE: _____ TIME: _____ DURATION OF VISIT: _____
HRS   MIN   SEC

PURPOSE FOR VISIT: ⬜ #1 ⬜ #2 ⬜ OTHER: _____ SUCCESS? ⬜ YES ⬜ NO

FAVORITE EUPHEMISM FOR PERFORMING #1:

FAVORITE RESTROOM GRAFFITI OR YOUR ORIGNAL DOODLE:

FAVORITE EUPHEMISM FOR PERFORMING #2:

WHILE YOU WERE HERE, DID YOU:
- ☐ TEXT SOMEONE
- ☐ MAKE A PHONE CALL
- ☐ EMAIL
- ☐ CHECK SOCIAL MEDIA
- ☐ TAKE A SELFIE
- ☐ LOOK IN THE MEDICINE CABINET
- ☐ CHECK YOUR TEETH
- ☐ CHECK OUT YOUR BUTT
- ☐ CHECK YOUR FLY
- ☐ READ
- ☐ FIX YOUR HAIR
- ☐ TAKE SOME EXTRA "ME TIME"
- ☐ TALK TO YOURSELF
- ☐ CONDUCT BUSINESS OTHER THAN YOUR "BUSINESS." CARE TO SHARE?
  _____

FAVORITE NAME FOR THIS ROOM:
- ☐ BATHROOM
- ☐ TOILET
- ☐ POWDER ROOM
- ☐ LAVATORY
- ☐ SHITTER
- ☐ LOO
- ☐ LITTLE GIRLS ROOM
- ☐ LITTLE BOYS ROOM
- ☐ COMFORT STATION
- ☐ OTHER: _____
- ☐ JOHN
- ☐ CAN
- ☐ HEAD
- ☐ POTTY
- ☐ CRAPPER
- ☐ WC

_____

RATINGS: 1 2 3 4 5
CLEANLINESS   ☆ ☆ ☆ ☆ ☆
AMBIENCE   ☆ ☆ ☆ ☆ ☆
AMENITIES   ☆ ☆ ☆ ☆ ☆
SOUND PROOFING   ☆ ☆ ☆ ☆ ☆
QUALITY OF THE FLUSH ☆ ☆ ☆ ☆ ☆
TOILET PAPER   ☆ ☆ ☆ ☆ ☆

OVERALL EXPERIENCE:
- ☐ BEST SEAT IN THE HOUSE ★ ★ ★ ★ ★
- ☐ WOULD POOP HERE AGAIN ★ ★ ★ ★
- ☐ SHIT GOT REAL ★ ★ ★
- ☐ SAME SHIT DIFFERENT HOUSE ★ ★
- ☐ THINGS JUST DIDN'T COME OUT RIGHT ★

THOUGHTS/MESSAGES: _____
_____
_____

Welcome! PLEASE SEAT YOURSELF AND ENJOY YOUR VISIT!

NAME: _____ DATE: _____ TIME: _____ DURATION OF VISIT: _____
HRS   MIN   SEC

PURPOSE FOR VISIT: ⬚ #1 ⬚ #2 ⬚ OTHER: _____ SUCCESS? ⬚ YES ⬚ NO

FAVORITE EUPHEMISM FOR PERFORMING #1:

FAVORITE EUPHEMISM FOR PERFORMING #2:

FAVORITE RESTROOM GRAFFITI OR YOUR ORIGNAL DOODLE:

WHILE YOU WERE HERE, DID YOU:
- ☐ TEXT SOMEONE
- ☐ MAKE A PHONE CALL
- ☐ EMAIL
- ☐ CHECK SOCIAL MEDIA
- ☐ TAKE A SELFIE
- ☐ LOOK IN THE MEDICINE CABINET
- ☐ CHECK YOUR TEETH
- ☐ CHECK OUT YOUR BUTT
- ☐ CHECK YOUR FLY
- ☐ READ
- ☐ FIX YOUR HAIR
- ☐ TAKE SOME EXTRA "ME TIME"
- ☐ TALK TO YOURSELF
- ☐ CONDUCT BUSINESS OTHER THAN YOUR "BUSINESS." CARE TO SHARE?

_____

FAVORITE NAME FOR THIS ROOM:
- ☐ BATHROOM
- ☐ TOILET
- ☐ POWDER ROOM
- ☐ LAVATORY
- ☐ SHITTER
- ☐ LOO
- ☐ LITTLE GIRLS ROOM
- ☐ LITTLE BOYS ROOM
- ☐ COMFORT STATION
- ☐ OTHER: _____
- ☐ JOHN
- ☐ CAN
- ☐ HEAD
- ☐ POTTY
- ☐ CRAPPER
- ☐ WC

_____

RATINGS: 1 2 3 4 5
CLEANLINESS   ☆ ☆ ☆ ☆ ☆
AMBIENCE   ☆ ☆ ☆ ☆ ☆
AMENITIES   ☆ ☆ ☆ ☆ ☆
SOUND PROOFING   ☆ ☆ ☆ ☆ ☆
QUALITY OF THE FLUSH ☆ ☆ ☆ ☆ ☆
TOILET PAPER   ☆ ☆ ☆ ☆ ☆

OVERALL EXPERIENCE:
- ☐ BEST SEAT IN THE HOUSE ★ ★ ★ ★ ★
- ☐ WOULD POOP HERE AGAIN ★ ★ ★ ★
- ☐ SHIT GOT REAL ★ ★ ★
- ☐ SAME SHIT DIFFERENT HOUSE ★ ★
- ☐ THINGS JUST DIDN'T COME OUT RIGHT ★

THOUGHTS/MESSAGES: _____
_____

Welcome! PLEASE SEAT YOURSELF AND ENJOY YOUR VISIT!

NAME: _____ DATE: _____ TIME: _____ DURATION OF VISIT: _____
HRS   MIN   SEC

PURPOSE FOR VISIT: 🧻 #1 🧻 #2 🧻 OTHER: _____ SUCCESS? 🧻 YES 🧻 NO

FAVORITE EUPHEMISM FOR PERFORMING #1:

FAVORITE RESTROOM GRAFFITI OR YOUR ORIGNAL DOODLE:

FAVORITE EUPHEMISM FOR PERFORMING #2:

WHILE YOU WERE HERE, DID YOU:
☐ TEXT SOMEONE
☐ MAKE A PHONE CALL
☐ EMAIL
☐ CHECK SOCIAL MEDIA
☐ TAKE A SELFIE
☐ LOOK IN THE MEDICINE CABINET
☐ CHECK YOUR TEETH
☐ CHECK OUT YOUR BUTT
☐ CHECK YOUR FLY
☐ READ
☐ FIX YOUR HAIR
☐ TAKE SOME EXTRA "ME TIME"
☐ TALK TO YOURSELF
☐ CONDUCT BUSINESS OTHER THAN YOUR "BUSINESS." CARE TO SHARE?
_____

FAVORITE NAME FOR THIS ROOM:
☐ BATHROOM   ☐ JOHN
☐ TOILET   ☐ CAN
☐ POWDER ROOM   ☐ HEAD
☐ LAVATORY   ☐ POTTY
☐ SHITTER   ☐ CRAPPER
☐ LOO   ☐ WC
☐ LITTLE GIRLS ROOM
☐ LITTLE BOYS ROOM
☐ COMFORT STATION
☐ OTHER: _____
_____

THOUGHTS/MESSAGES: _____
_____
_____

RATINGS:
	1	2	3	4	5
CLEANLINESS	☆	☆	☆	☆	☆
AMBIENCE	☆	☆	☆	☆	☆
AMENITIES	☆	☆	☆	☆	☆
SOUND PROOFING	☆	☆	☆	☆	☆
QUALITY OF THE FLUSH	☆	☆	☆	☆	☆
TOILET PAPER	☆	☆	☆	☆	☆

OVERALL EXPERIENCE:
☐ BEST SEAT IN THE HOUSE ★ ★ ★ ★ ★
☐ WOULD POOP HERE AGAIN ★ ★ ★ ★
☐ SHIT GOT REAL ★ ★ ★
☐ SAME SHIT DIFFERENT HOUSE ★ ★
☐ THINGS JUST DIDN'T COME OUT RIGHT ★

Welcome! PLEASE SEAT YOURSELF AND ENJOY YOUR VISIT!

NAME: _____ DATE: _____ TIME: _____ DURATION OF VISIT: _____

HRS   MIN   SEC

PURPOSE FOR VISIT: ☐ #1 ☐ #2 ☐ OTHER: _____ SUCCESS? ☐ YES ☐ NO

FAVORITE EUPHEMISM FOR PERFORMING #1:

FAVORITE RESTROOM GRAFFITI OR YOUR ORIGNAL DOODLE:

FAVORITE EUPHEMISM FOR PERFORMING #2:

WHILE YOU WERE HERE, DID YOU:
☐ TEXT SOMEONE
☐ MAKE A PHONE CALL
☐ EMAIL
☐ CHECK SOCIAL MEDIA
☐ TAKE A SELFIE
☐ LOOK IN THE MEDICINE CABINET
☐ CHECK YOUR TEETH
☐ CHECK OUT YOUR BUTT
☐ CHECK YOUR FLY
☐ READ
☐ FIX YOUR HAIR
☐ TAKE SOME EXTRA "ME TIME"
☐ TALK TO YOURSELF
☐ CONDUCT BUSINESS OTHER THAN YOUR "BUSINESS." CARE TO SHARE?

FAVORITE NAME FOR THIS ROOM:
☐ BATHROOM   ☐ JOHN
☐ TOILET   ☐ CAN
☐ POWDER ROOM ☐ HEAD
☐ LAVATORY   ☐ POTTY
☐ SHITTER   ☐ CRAPPER
☐ LOO   ☐ WC
☐ LITTLE GIRLS ROOM
☐ LITTLE BOYS ROOM
☐ COMFORT STATION
☐ OTHER: _____

RATINGS:

	1	2	3	4	5
CLEANLINESS	☆	☆	☆	☆	☆
AMBIENCE	☆	☆	☆	☆	☆
AMENITIES	☆	☆	☆	☆	☆
SOUND PROOFING	☆	☆	☆	☆	☆
QUALITY OF THE FLUSH	☆	☆	☆	☆	☆
TOILET PAPER	☆	☆	☆	☆	☆

OVERALL EXPERIENCE:
☐ BEST SEAT IN THE HOUSE ★ ★ ★ ★ ★
☐ WOULD POOP HERE AGAIN ★ ★ ★ ★
☐ SHIT GOT REAL ★ ★ ★
☐ SAME SHIT DIFFERENT HOUSE ★ ★
☐ THINGS JUST DIDN'T COME OUT RIGHT ★

THOUGHTS/MESSAGES: _____

Welcome! PLEASE SEAT YOURSELF AND ENJOY YOUR VISIT!

NAME: _____ DATE: _____ TIME: _____ DURATION OF VISIT: _____
HRS   MIN   SEC

PURPOSE FOR VISIT: 🧻 #1   🧻 #2   🧻 OTHER: _____   SUCCESS? 🧻 YES 🧻 NO

FAVORITE EUPHEMISM FOR PERFORMING #1:

FAVORITE RESTROOM GRAFFITI OR YOUR ORIGNAL DOODLE:

FAVORITE EUPHEMISM FOR PERFORMING #2:

WHILE YOU WERE HERE, DID YOU:
- ☐ TEXT SOMEONE
- ☐ MAKE A PHONE CALL
- ☐ EMAIL
- ☐ CHECK SOCIAL MEDIA
- ☐ TAKE A SELFIE
- ☐ LOOK IN THE MEDICINE CABINET
- ☐ CHECK YOUR TEETH
- ☐ CHECK OUT YOUR BUTT
- ☐ CHECK YOUR FLY
- ☐ READ
- ☐ FIX YOUR HAIR
- ☐ TAKE SOME EXTRA "ME TIME"
- ☐ TALK TO YOURSELF
- ☐ CONDUCT BUSINESS OTHER THAN YOUR "BUSINESS." CARE TO SHARE?
  _____

FAVORITE NAME FOR THIS ROOM:
- ☐ BATHROOM
- ☐ TOILET
- ☐ POWDER ROOM
- ☐ LAVATORY
- ☐ SHITTER
- ☐ LOO
- ☐ LITTLE GIRLS ROOM
- ☐ LITTLE BOYS ROOM
- ☐ COMFORT STATION
- ☐ OTHER: _____
- ☐ JOHN
- ☐ CAN
- ☐ HEAD
- ☐ POTTY
- ☐ CRAPPER
- ☐ WC

_____

THOUGHTS/MESSAGES: _____
_____
_____

RATINGS: 1 2 3 4 5
CLEANLINESS   ☆ ☆ ☆ ☆ ☆
AMBIENCE   ☆ ☆ ☆ ☆ ☆
AMENITIES   ☆ ☆ ☆ ☆ ☆
SOUND PROOFING   ☆ ☆ ☆ ☆ ☆
QUALITY OF THE FLUSH   ☆ ☆ ☆ ☆ ☆
TOILET PAPER   ☆ ☆ ☆ ☆ ☆

OVERALL EXPERIENCE:
- ☐ BEST SEAT IN THE HOUSE   ★ ★ ★ ★ ★
- ☐ WOULD POOP HERE AGAIN   ★ ★ ★ ★
- ☐ SHIT GOT REAL   ★ ★ ★
- ☐ SAME SHIT DIFFERENT HOUSE   ★ ★
- ☐ THINGS JUST DIDN'T COME OUT RIGHT ★

Welcome! PLEASE SEAT YOURSELF AND ENJOY YOUR VISIT!

NAME: _____ DATE: _____ TIME: _____ DURATION OF VISIT: _____
                                                                              HRS   MIN   SEC

PURPOSE FOR VISIT: 🧻 #1 🧻 #2 🧻 OTHER: _____ SUCCESS? 🧻 YES 🧻 NO

FAVORITE EUPHEMISM FOR PERFORMING #1:

FAVORITE RESTROOM GRAFFITI OR YOUR ORIGNAL DOODLE:

FAVORITE EUPHEMISM FOR PERFORMING #2:

WHILE YOU WERE HERE, DID YOU:

TEXT SOMEONE
MAKE A PHONE CALL
EMAIL
CHECK SOCIAL MEDIA
TAKE A SELFIE
LOOK IN THE MEDICINE CABINET
CHECK YOUR TEETH
CHECK OUT YOUR BUTT
CHECK YOUR FLY
READ
FIX YOUR HAIR
TAKE SOME EXTRA "ME TIME"
TALK TO YOURSELF
CONDUCT BUSINESS OTHER THAN
YOUR "BUSINESS." CARE TO SHARE?
_____

FAVORITE NAME FOR THIS ROOM:

☐ BATHROOM   ☐ JOHN
☐ TOILET   ☐ CAN
☐ POWDER ROOM   ☐ HEAD
☐ LAVATORY   ☐ POTTY
☐ SHITTER   ☐ CRAPPER
☐ LOO   ☐ WC
☐ LITTLE GIRLS ROOM
☐ LITTLE BOYS ROOM
☐ COMFORT STATION
☐ OTHER: _____
_____

RATINGS: 1 2 3 4 5
CLEANLINESS   ☆ ☆ ☆ ☆ ☆
AMBIENCE   ☆ ☆ ☆ ☆ ☆
AMENITIES   ☆ ☆ ☆ ☆ ☆
SOUND PROOFING   ☆ ☆ ☆ ☆ ☆
QUALITY OF THE FLUSH   ☆ ☆ ☆ ☆ ☆
TOILET PAPER   ☆ ☆ ☆ ☆ ☆

OVERALL EXPERIENCE:
☐ BEST SEAT IN THE HOUSE   ★ ★ ★ ★ ★
☐ WOULD POOP HERE AGAIN   ★ ★ ★ ★
☐ SHIT GOT REAL   ★ ★ ★
☐ SAME SHIT DIFFERENT HOUSE   ★ ★
☐ THINGS JUST DIDN'T COME OUT RIGHT   ★

THOUGHTS/MESSAGES: _____
_____
_____

Welcome! PLEASE SEAT YOURSELF AND ENJOY YOUR VISIT!

NAME: _____ DATE: _____ TIME: _____ DURATION OF VISIT: _____

HRS   MIN   SEC

PURPOSE FOR VISIT: ☐ #1 ☐ #2 ☐ OTHER: _____ SUCCESS? ☐ YES ☐ NO

FAVORITE EUPHEMISM FOR PERFORMING #1: | FAVORITE RESTROOM GRAFFITI OR YOUR ORIGNAL DOODLE:

FAVORITE EUPHEMISM FOR PERFORMING #2:

WHILE YOU WERE HERE, DID YOU:
- ☐ TEXT SOMEONE
- ☐ MAKE A PHONE CALL
- ☐ EMAIL
- ☐ CHECK SOCIAL MEDIA
- ☐ TAKE A SELFIE
- ☐ LOOK IN THE MEDICINE CABINET
- ☐ CHECK YOUR TEETH
- ☐ CHECK OUT YOUR BUTT
- ☐ CHECK YOUR FLY
- ☐ READ
- ☐ FIX YOUR HAIR
- ☐ TAKE SOME EXTRA "ME TIME"
- ☐ TALK TO YOURSELF
- ☐ CONDUCT BUSINESS OTHER THAN YOUR "BUSINESS." CARE TO SHARE?

FAVORITE NAME FOR THIS ROOM:
- ☐ BATHROOM
- ☐ TOILET
- ☐ POWDER ROOM
- ☐ LAVATORY
- ☐ SHITTER
- ☐ LOO
- ☐ LITTLE GIRLS ROOM
- ☐ LITTLE BOYS ROOM
- ☐ COMFORT STATION
- ☐ OTHER: _____

- ☐ JOHN
- ☐ CAN
- ☐ HEAD
- ☐ POTTY
- ☐ CRAPPER
- ☐ WC

RATINGS:

	1 2 3 4 5
CLEANLINESS	☆ ☆ ☆ ☆ ☆
AMBIENCE	☆ ☆ ☆ ☆ ☆
AMENITIES	☆ ☆ ☆ ☆ ☆
SOUND PROOFING	☆ ☆ ☆ ☆ ☆
QUALITY OF THE FLUSH	☆ ☆ ☆ ☆ ☆
TOILET PAPER	☆ ☆ ☆ ☆ ☆

OVERALL EXPERIENCE:
- ☐ BEST SEAT IN THE HOUSE ★ ★ ★ ★ ★
- ☐ WOULD POOP HERE AGAIN ★ ★ ★ ★
- ☐ SHIT GOT REAL ★ ★ ★
- ☐ SAME SHIT DIFFERENT HOUSE ★ ★
- ☐ THINGS JUST DIDN'T COME OUT RIGHT ★

THOUGHTS/MESSAGES: _____

Welcome! PLEASE SEAT YOURSELF AND ENJOY YOUR VISIT!

NAME: _____ DATE: _____ TIME: _____ DURATION OF VISIT: _____

HRS   MIN   SEC

PURPOSE FOR VISIT: ▢ #1 ▢ #2 ▢ OTHER: _____ SUCCESS? ▢ YES ▢ NO

FAVORITE EUPHEMISM FOR PERFORMING #1:

FAVORITE RESTROOM GRAFFITI OR YOUR ORIGNAL DOODLE:

FAVORITE EUPHEMISM FOR PERFORMING #2:

WHILE YOU WERE HERE, DID YOU:
▢ TEXT SOMEONE
▢ MAKE A PHONE CALL
▢ EMAIL
▢ CHECK SOCIAL MEDIA
▢ TAKE A SELFIE
▢ LOOK IN THE MEDICINE CABINET
▢ CHECK YOUR TEETH
▢ CHECK OUT YOUR BUTT
▢ CHECK YOUR FLY
▢ READ
▢ FIX YOUR HAIR
▢ TAKE SOME EXTRA "ME TIME"
▢ TALK TO YOURSELF
▢ CONDUCT BUSINESS OTHER THAN YOUR "BUSINESS." CARE TO SHARE?
_____

FAVORITE NAME FOR THIS ROOM:
▢ BATHROOM
▢ TOILET
▢ POWDER ROOM
▢ LAVATORY
▢ SHITTER
▢ LOO
▢ LITTLE GIRLS ROOM
▢ LITTLE BOYS ROOM
▢ COMFORT STATION
▢ OTHER: _____
▢ JOHN
▢ CAN
▢ HEAD
▢ POTTY
▢ CRAPPER
▢ WC

_____

RATINGS:

	1	2	3	4	5
CLEANLINESS	☆	☆	☆	☆	☆
AMBIENCE	☆	☆	☆	☆	☆
AMENITIES	☆	☆	☆	☆	☆
SOUND PROOFING	☆	☆	☆	☆	☆
QUALITY OF THE FLUSH	☆	☆	☆	☆	☆
TOILET PAPER	☆	☆	☆	☆	☆

OVERALL EXPERIENCE:
▢ BEST SEAT IN THE HOUSE ★ ★ ★ ★ ★
▢ WOULD POOP HERE AGAIN ★ ★ ★ ★
▢ SHIT GOT REAL ★ ★ ★
▢ SAME SHIT DIFFERENT HOUSE ★ ★
▢ THINGS JUST DIDN'T COME OUT RIGHT ★

THOUGHTS/MESSAGES: _____
_____
_____

Welcome! PLEASE SEAT YOURSELF AND ENJOY YOUR VISIT!

NAME: _____ DATE: _____ TIME: _____ DURATION OF VISIT: _____
                                                                                HRS   MIN   SEC

PURPOSE FOR VISIT: ☐ #1 ☐ #2 ☐ OTHER: _____ SUCCESS? ☐ YES ☐ NO

FAVORITE EUPHEMISM FOR PERFORMING #1:   FAVORITE RESTROOM GRAFFITI OR YOUR ORIGNAL DOODLE:

FAVORITE EUPHEMISM FOR PERFORMING #2:

WHILE YOU WERE HERE, DID YOU:
☐ TEXT SOMEONE
☐ MAKE A PHONE CALL
☐ EMAIL
☐ CHECK SOCIAL MEDIA
☐ TAKE A SELFIE
☐ LOOK IN THE MEDICINE CABINET
☐ CHECK YOUR TEETH
☐ CHECK OUT YOUR BUTT
☐ CHECK YOUR FLY
☐ READ
☐ FIX YOUR HAIR
☐ TAKE SOME EXTRA "ME TIME"
☐ TALK TO YOURSELF
☐ CONDUCT BUSINESS OTHER THAN
  YOUR "BUSINESS." CARE TO SHARE?
_____

FAVORITE NAME FOR THIS ROOM:
☐ BATHROOM   ☐ JOHN
☐ TOILET   ☐ CAN
☐ POWDER ROOM   ☐ HEAD
☐ LAVATORY   ☐ POTTY
☐ SHITTER   ☐ CRAPPER
☐ LOO   ☐ WC
☐ LITTLE GIRLS ROOM
☐ LITTLE BOYS ROOM
☐ COMFORT STATION
☐ OTHER: _____
_____

THOUGHTS/MESSAGES: _____
_____
_____

RATINGS:

	1	2	3	4	5
CLEANLINESS	☆	☆	☆	☆	☆
AMBIENCE	☆	☆	☆	☆	☆
AMENITIES	☆	☆	☆	☆	☆
SOUND PROOFING	☆	☆	☆	☆	☆
QUALITY OF THE FLUSH	☆	☆	☆	☆	☆
TOILET PAPER	☆	☆	☆	☆	☆

OVERALL EXPERIENCE:
☐ BEST SEAT IN THE HOUSE   ★ ★ ★ ★ ★
☐ WOULD POOP HERE AGAIN   ★ ★ ★ ★
☐ SHIT GOT REAL   ★ ★ ★
☐ SAME SHIT DIFFERENT HOUSE   ★ ★
☐ THINGS JUST DIDN'T COME OUT RIGHT ★

Welcome! PLEASE SEAT YOURSELF AND ENJOY YOUR VISIT!

NAME: _____ DATE: _____ TIME: _____ DURATION OF VISIT: _____

HRS   MIN   SEC

PURPOSE FOR VISIT: ▢ #1 ▢ #2 ▢ OTHER: _____ SUCCESS? ▢ YES ▢ NO

FAVORITE EUPHEMISM FOR PERFORMING #1:

FAVORITE RESTROOM GRAFFITI OR YOUR ORIGNAL DOODLE:

FAVORITE EUPHEMISM FOR PERFORMING #2:

WHILE YOU WERE HERE, DID YOU:
▢ TEXT SOMEONE
▢ MAKE A PHONE CALL
▢ EMAIL
▢ CHECK SOCIAL MEDIA
▢ TAKE A SELFIE
▢ LOOK IN THE MEDICINE CABINET
▢ CHECK YOUR TEETH
▢ CHECK OUT YOUR BUTT
▢ CHECK YOUR FLY
▢ READ
▢ FIX YOUR HAIR
▢ TAKE SOME EXTRA "ME TIME"
▢ TALK TO YOURSELF
▢ CONDUCT BUSINESS OTHER THAN YOUR "BUSINESS." CARE TO SHARE?
_____

FAVORITE NAME FOR THIS ROOM:
▢ BATHROOM
▢ TOILET
▢ POWDER ROOM
▢ LAVATORY
▢ SHITTER
▢ LOO
▢ LITTLE GIRLS ROOM
▢ LITTLE BOYS ROOM
▢ COMFORT STATION
▢ OTHER: _____
▢ JOHN
▢ CAN
▢ HEAD
▢ POTTY
▢ CRAPPER
▢ WC

_____

THOUGHTS/MESSAGES: _____
_____
_____

RATINGS: 1 2 3 4 5
CLEANLINESS   ☆ ☆ ☆ ☆ ☆
AMBIENCE   ☆ ☆ ☆ ☆ ☆
AMENITIES   ☆ ☆ ☆ ☆ ☆
SOUND PROOFING   ☆ ☆ ☆ ☆ ☆
QUALITY OF THE FLUSH ☆ ☆ ☆ ☆ ☆
TOILET PAPER   ☆ ☆ ☆ ☆ ☆

OVERALL EXPERIENCE:
▢ BEST SEAT IN THE HOUSE   ★ ★ ★ ★ ★
▢ WOULD POOP HERE AGAIN   ★ ★ ★ ★
▢ SHIT GOT REAL   ★ ★ ★
▢ SAME SHIT DIFFERENT HOUSE   ★ ★
▢ THINGS JUST DIDN'T COME OUT RIGHT   ★

Welcome! PLEASE SEAT YOURSELF AND ENJOY YOUR VISIT!

NAME: _____ DATE: _____ TIME: _____ DURATION OF VISIT: _____
HRS   MIN   SEC

PURPOSE FOR VISIT: 🧻 #1 🧻 #2 🧻 OTHER: _____ SUCCESS? 🧻 YES 🧻 NO

FAVORITE EUPHEMISM FOR PERFORMING #1:

FAVORITE RESTROOM GRAFFITI OR YOUR ORIGNAL DOODLE:

FAVORITE EUPHEMISM FOR PERFORMING #2:

WHILE YOU WERE HERE, DID YOU:
- ☐ TEXT SOMEONE
- ☐ MAKE A PHONE CALL
- ☐ EMAIL
- ☐ CHECK SOCIAL MEDIA
- ☐ TAKE A SELFIE
- ☐ LOOK IN THE MEDICINE CABINET
- ☐ CHECK YOUR TEETH
- ☐ CHECK OUT YOUR BUTT
- ☐ CHECK YOUR FLY
- ☐ READ
- ☐ FIX YOUR HAIR
- ☐ TAKE SOME EXTRA "ME TIME"
- ☐ TALK TO YOURSELF
- ☐ CONDUCT BUSINESS OTHER THAN YOUR "BUSINESS." CARE TO SHARE?

FAVORITE NAME FOR THIS ROOM:
- ☐ BATHROOM
- ☐ TOILET
- ☐ POWDER ROOM
- ☐ LAVATORY
- ☐ SHITTER
- ☐ LOO
- ☐ LITTLE GIRLS ROOM
- ☐ LITTLE BOYS ROOM
- ☐ COMFORT STATION
- ☐ OTHER: _____
- ☐ JOHN
- ☐ CAN
- ☐ HEAD
- ☐ POTTY
- ☐ CRAPPER
- ☐ WC

RATINGS:
	1	2	3	4	5
CLEANLINESS	☆	☆	☆	☆	☆
AMBIENCE	☆	☆	☆	☆	☆
AMENITIES	☆	☆	☆	☆	☆
SOUND PROOFING	☆	☆	☆	☆	☆
QUALITY OF THE FLUSH	☆	☆	☆	☆	☆
TOILET PAPER	☆	☆	☆	☆	☆

OVERALL EXPERIENCE:
- ☐ BEST SEAT IN THE HOUSE ★ ★ ★ ★ ★
- ☐ WOULD POOP HERE AGAIN ★ ★ ★ ★
- ☐ SHIT GOT REAL ★ ★ ★
- ☐ SAME SHIT DIFFERENT HOUSE ★ ★
- ☐ THINGS JUST DIDN'T COME OUT RIGHT ★

THOUGHTS/MESSAGES: _____

Welcome! PLEASE SEAT YOURSELF AND ENJOY YOUR VISIT!

NAME: _____ DATE: _____ TIME: _____ DURATION OF VISIT: _____

HRS   MIN   SEC

PURPOSE FOR VISIT: ☐ #1 ☐ #2 ☐ OTHER: _____ SUCCESS? ☐ YES ☐ NO

FAVORITE EUPHEMISM FOR PERFORMING #1: | FAVORITE RESTROOM GRAFFITI OR YOUR ORIGNAL DOODLE:

FAVORITE EUPHEMISM FOR PERFORMING #2:

WHILE YOU WERE HERE, DID YOU:
☐ TEXT SOMEONE
☐ MAKE A PHONE CALL
☐ EMAIL
☐ CHECK SOCIAL MEDIA
☐ TAKE A SELFIE
☐ LOOK IN THE MEDICINE CABINET
☐ CHECK YOUR TEETH
☐ CHECK OUT YOUR BUTT
☐ CHECK YOUR FLY
☐ READ
☐ FIX YOUR HAIR
☐ TAKE SOME EXTRA "ME TIME"
☐ TALK TO YOURSELF
☐ CONDUCT BUSINESS OTHER THAN YOUR "BUSINESS." CARE TO SHARE?

FAVORITE NAME FOR THIS ROOM:
☐ BATHROOM   ☐ JOHN
☐ TOILET   ☐ CAN
☐ POWDER ROOM   ☐ HEAD
☐ LAVATORY   ☐ POTTY
☐ SHITTER   ☐ CRAPPER
☐ LOO   ☐ WC
☐ LITTLE GIRLS ROOM
☐ LITTLE BOYS ROOM
☐ COMFORT STATION
☐ OTHER: _____

_____

THOUGHTS/MESSAGES: _____

_____

_____

RATINGS:

	1	2	3	4	5
CLEANLINESS	☆	☆	☆	☆	☆
AMBIENCE	☆	☆	☆	☆	☆
AMENITIES	☆	☆	☆	☆	☆
SOUND PROOFING	☆	☆	☆	☆	☆
QUALITY OF THE FLUSH	☆	☆	☆	☆	☆
TOILET PAPER	☆	☆	☆	☆	☆

OVERALL EXPERIENCE:
☐ BEST SEAT IN THE HOUSE   ★ ★ ★ ★ ★
☐ WOULD POOP HERE AGAIN   ★ ★ ★ ★
☐ SHIT GOT REAL   ★ ★ ★
☐ SAME SHIT DIFFERENT HOUSE   ★ ★
☐ THINGS JUST DIDN'T COME OUT RIGHT   ★

Welcome! PLEASE SEAT YOURSELF AND ENJOY YOUR VISIT!

NAME: _____ DATE: _____ TIME: _____ DURATION OF VISIT: _____
HRS   MIN   SEC

PURPOSE FOR VISIT: ☐ #1 ☐ #2 ☐ OTHER: _____ SUCCESS? ☐ YES ☐ NO

FAVORITE EUPHEMISM FOR PERFORMING #1:

FAVORITE EUPHEMISM FOR PERFORMING #2:

FAVORITE RESTROOM GRAFFITI OR YOUR ORIGNAL DOODLE:

WHILE YOU WERE HERE, DID YOU:
- ☐ TEXT SOMEONE
- ☐ MAKE A PHONE CALL
- ☐ EMAIL
- ☐ CHECK SOCIAL MEDIA
- ☐ TAKE A SELFIE
- ☐ LOOK IN THE MEDICINE CABINET
- ☐ CHECK YOUR TEETH
- ☐ CHECK OUT YOUR BUTT
- ☐ CHECK YOUR FLY
- ☐ READ
- ☐ FIX YOUR HAIR
- ☐ TAKE SOME EXTRA "ME TIME"
- ☐ TALK TO YOURSELF
- ☐ CONDUCT BUSINESS OTHER THAN YOUR "BUSINESS." CARE TO SHARE?
  _____

FAVORITE NAME FOR THIS ROOM:
- ☐ BATHROOM
- ☐ TOILET
- ☐ POWDER ROOM
- ☐ LAVATORY
- ☐ SHITTER
- ☐ LOO
- ☐ LITTLE GIRLS ROOM
- ☐ LITTLE BOYS ROOM
- ☐ COMFORT STATION
- ☐ OTHER: _____

- ☐ JOHN
- ☐ CAN
- ☐ HEAD
- ☐ POTTY
- ☐ CRAPPER
- ☐ WC

_____

RATINGS:	1	2	3	4	5
CLEANLINESS	☆	☆	☆	☆	☆
AMBIENCE	☆	☆	☆	☆	☆
AMENITIES	☆	☆	☆	☆	☆
SOUND PROOFING	☆	☆	☆	☆	☆
QUALITY OF THE FLUSH	☆	☆	☆	☆	☆
TOILET PAPER	☆	☆	☆	☆	☆

OVERALL EXPERIENCE:
- ☐ BEST SEAT IN THE HOUSE ★ ★ ★ ★ ★
- ☐ WOULD POOP HERE AGAIN ★ ★ ★ ★
- ☐ SHIT GOT REAL ★ ★ ★
- ☐ SAME SHIT DIFFERENT HOUSE ★ ★
- ☐ THINGS JUST DIDN'T COME OUT RIGHT ★

THOUGHTS/MESSAGES: _____
_____
_____

Made in the USA
Coppell, TX
13 June 2022

78760011R20057